Aeschylus: Prom

COMPANIONS TO
GREEK AND ROMAN TRAGEDY

Series editor: Thomas Harrison

Aeschylus: Agamemnon Barbara Goward
Aeschylus: Eumenides Robin Mitchell-Boyask
Aeschylus: Persians David Rosenbloom
Aeschylus: Prometheus Bound I.A. Ruffell
Aeschylus: Seven Against Thebes Isabelle Torrance
Aeschylus: Suppliants Thalia Papadopoulou
Euripides: Bacchae Sophie Mills
Euripides: Heracles Emma Griffiths
Euripides: Hippolytus Sophie Mills
Euripides: Ion Lorna Swift
Euripides: Iphigenia at Aulis Pantelis Michelakis
Euripides: Medea William Allan
Euripides: Orestes Matthew Wright
Euripides: Phoenician Women Thalia Papadopoulou
Euripides: Suppliant Women Ian Storey
Euripides: Trojan Women Barbara Goff
Seneca: Phaedra Roland Mayer
Seneca: Thyestes Peter Davis
Sophocles: Ajax Jon Hesk
Sophocles: Electra Michael Lloyd
Sophocles: Oedipus at Colonus Adrian Kelly
Sophocles: Philoctetes Hanna Roisman
Sophocles: Women of Trachis Brad Levett

COMPANIONS TO
GREEK AND ROMAN TRAGEDY

Aeschylus:
Prometheus Bound

I.A. Ruffell

Georg Bull Andersen.

Bristol Classical Press

First published in 2012 by
Bristol Classical Press
an imprint of
Bloomsbury Academic
Bloomsbury Publishing Plc
50 Bedford Square,
London WC1B 3DP, UK

CIP records for this book are available from the
British Library and the Library of Congress

ISBN 978 0 7156 3476 9

Typeset by Ray Davies
Printed and bound in Great Britain by
CPI Group (UK) Ltd, Croydon, Surrey

www.bloomsburyacademic.com

Contents

Preface

The origins of this book lie in a conversation with Shomit Dutta. I would like to thank Deborah Blake, at Bloomsbury Academic, and the series editor, Tom Harrison, not least for their patience.

I have learnt a great deal about *Prometheus Bound* from discussing it with colleagues, particularly Alex Garvie, Lisa Hau, Julia Shear and Catherine Steel, and from my students, particularly all those who have discussed the play with me as part of their MLitt option in Greek Tragedy.

Prometheus Bound is given in its usual English translated title; in other publications it is frequently abbreviated as *PV* (for its Latin form, *Prometheus Vinctus*) or, less often, known as *Prometheus Desmotes*, its transliterated Greek form. *Prometheus Unbound* is elsewhere seen as *Prometheus Lyomenos*, its transliterated Greek form. Aeschylus' *Libation Bearers* is often elsewhere seen as *Choephori*, in a latinised form of its Greek title.

Comic fragments are cited from Kassel and Austin; tragic fragments from the edition of Snell, Kannicht and Radt, except for additional fragments of *Prometheus Unbound* given by Griffith in his edition; historians and mythographers from Jacoby; presocratic philosophers and sophists from Diels-Kranz; iambic and elegiac fragments from West. All translations are my own. Greek is transliterated, not latinised, with *kh* for chi, but *y* for upsilon. Long *ê* and *ô* are marked. Greek proper names are given in transliterated form (without the marking of quantity) except where there is an English form in common use (Aeschylus, Homer, Plato).

Dates under 1000 are all BCE, dates above 1400 are all CE.

1

Themes, Contexts and Receptions

According to the erstwhile classical scholar and occasional literary critic Karl Marx, the Titan Prometheus is 'the most eminent saint and martyr in the philosophical calendar'.[1] This provocative claim applied specifically to the Prometheus of Aeschylus' *Prometheus Bound*. It is not hard to see why Marx found the Aeschylean figure so enticing. Prometheus: stealer of fire, symbol of progress in an unforgiving world, opponent of tyrannical gods (if not religion itself), architect of shared knowledge, openness and human achievement – what self-respecting revolutionary could resist? The play itself is a clarion cry for self-confident and optimistic human action, marrying technological self-improvement and resistance to personal and political oppression.

Marx himself may not be the most ideal guide to classical antiquity, but in the case of *Prometheus Bound*, at least, he is joined by a formidable array of radical artists – from the puritan Milton, through the Romantics Goethe and Percy Shelley to experimental twentieth-century music and the documentation of deindustrialisation, while popular culture and radical politics on both left and right have been busily appropriating Prometheus. The image of Prometheus looms large over the genre of science fiction, filtered through Mary Shelley's *Frankenstein*, provocatively subtitled *The Modern Prometheus*.

With such a roster of intertexts, *Prometheus Bound* is among the most influential of surviving Greek tragedies. Perhaps the only real rival is Sophokles' *Oedipus Tyrannus*, thanks to an unholy alliance of Aristotle and Freud, which canonised that

7

play as both the archetype of tragic plot and a foundational text for psychoanalysis. The polarity between *Prometheus Bound* and *Oedipus Tyrannus* embodies the twin demands of Greek tragedy, for social and political action and for psychological understanding.

That is, outside the academy. The prime area of concern for professional classicists has been a long-running debate as to whether the play is by Aeschylus at all, in whole or in part. The qualities that have appealed to major poets, novelists and musicians have been widely derided in academic textbooks. Nowhere is there an instance of such a clearly bifurcated reception of a classical text.

One reason is that *Prometheus Bound*'s take on politics and religion – its philosophical position, if we follow Marx – makes many modern critics deeply uncomfortable. Indeed, for one critic, the major stumbling block is the (undeniable) fact that the play is deeply and unambiguously political. Another critic sees the treatment of religion as unconscionable – for him, the play is 'irreligious'.[2] This upsets many tidy modern constructions of 'Aeschylus': he is just not supposed to do that sort of thing. The doubts go deeper than biography alone. For critics wedded to notions of the autonomy of literature, blatant political interventions and borderline religious scepticism are not supposed to happen in a tragedy. The politics of the play are also deeply unfashionable. With the move in the past twenty to thirty years towards historical and political readings of Greek tragedy, *Prometheus Bound* has not figured strongly in the discussion. Its explicit political engagement and grand narrative of progress are unambiguous, but its defiance, optimism and apparent lack of cynicism and irony are out of touch with the postmodern times. It is not a play about identity, the local and the particular, but blatantly puts political ideas on the grand, universalising stage. As with most Greek tragedies, a very precise political intervention is difficult to observe, but its cosmic and human politics would certainly have resonated in their original performance context.

Prometheus Bound packs a punch in formal as well as thematic terms. Although there are many exceptions to modern generalisations about the form of tragedy, *Prometheus Bound* confounds categories. Its staging is the most grandstanding and spectacular of surviving plays, and its plot is not at all conventional. It is situated almost entirely on the divine plane and is deeply episodic, dominated by long speeches as Prometheus, pinned to his rock, interacts with visitors. Not much actually happens within the time of the play. This upsets many critics working in an Aristotelian tradition, where plot and the example of *Oedipus Tyrannus* are paramount. Tragic plots are in fact many and various, but the notion that a tragedy should involve a human protagonist from a decent family, making a mistake (*hamartia*) and undergoing *peripeteia* (reversal) and *anagnôrisis* (recognition) dies very hard indeed. And in terms of emotion, there is a feeling that although there is plenty of suffering on the part of Prometheus, there is altogether too much defiance and his regrets far too few to mention.

Neither Aeschylus in general nor *Prometheus Bound* in particular were favoured by neo-classical theatre, which followed a rather simplified view of Aristotelian principles. Nor does *Prometheus Bound* feature prominently amongst the output of major (institutional, national) theatre companies or university drama (another common venue for productions of classical plays). The broadening of modes of performance in the twentieth century have seen the play adopted by experimental and political theatre. It flourishes in less conventional settings: multimedia projects and science fiction, in addition to the assorted radical writers and misfits mentioned above. That said, the play is far from uncomplicated in its handling of time and space, and its flash-backs and flash-forwards are intimately bound up with its politics and its personalities. Unlike many or most other Greek tragedies, where the storyline was well known, there are genuine surprises. The preponderance of speech (and song) over action is similar to other Aeschylean plays: *Seven Against Thebes* (discounting the ending), *Suppliant Women* or even *Agamemnon*. Post-Brechtian theatre has in many ways taken us back closer to the style of earlier Greek tragedy. For Prometheus chained to his rock, think, perhaps, of Marat in his bathtub in Peter Weiss' *Marat/Sade*.[3]

The debate over authorship can help to establish the date and context of the play, but it is important to clarify what is at stake in that discussion. For many critics, there is an implicit judgment of quality (it's a bad play, therefore un-Aeschylean), or inference of quality (it is Aeschylean, therefore worth studying). Arguments around the edge of Shakespeare's canon are in some respects similar, although no Shakespearean play has been ejected quite so forcibly from the canon. I hope to persuade readers that *Prometheus Bound* has rightly been thought worth reading and performing, regardless of author. In any case, we know so little reliably about ancient dramatists that there can be no serious attempt at biographical criticism, even with plays whose authorship is uncontroversial. Our inherited idea of 'Aeschylus' depends on the play's traditional ascription. Even if a pastiche of Aeschylus, *Prometheus Bound* has been informing the idea of Aeschylus since the fourth century BCE and perhaps earlier.

The broad outline of the book is as follows. I consider date, authorship and historical context in the rest of this chapter. Detailed consideration of the play begins in Chapter 2 with the confrontation on the divine plane between Zeus, tyrant and frustrated genocide, and Prometheus, Titan and friend of humankind. I will examine Zeus' rise to power, the characterisation of his rule, his treatment of erstwhile allies and exemplary victims. I will consider, with Milton and the Shelleys, how this cosmic drama can be related to the human scale, and particularly how *Prometheus Bound* would have played in fifth-century Athens.

In Chapter 3, I focus on the central area of tension in the play – knowledge and the access to knowledge. I show how *Prometheus Bound* confronts earlier pessimistic accounts of human development and elbows them aside in favour of a much more optimistic and progressive perspective. I discuss how the play engages with developing intellectual movements of the period and makes an intervention which links progressive politics with access to and ownership of knowledge. I also ask how developments in a further play or plays might have affected the political concerns of the drama.

Chapter 4 examines the play's emphasis on spectacle and the problems and possibilities in its original staging. The play's self-consciousness of its display of pain encourages the audience to reflect upon their emotional engagement with the play, but tempers idealism with a reserve about masculinity and the individual activist. I also consider the other major formal feature of the play, its use of narrative in extended speech and solo song (monody), particularly the temporal and spatial implications of such narratives in the scene between Io and Prometheus.

Finally, in Chapter 5, I turn explicitly to literary and non-literary receptions and consider how they inform a reading of the play. I discuss the re-emergence of *Prometheus Bound*, its serial use by Milton in exploring the relationship between human and divine, and between freedom and authority; the rebellion against religion and championing of the individual by the Romantics; the reintroduction of a materialist, scientific edge in Mary Shelley's *Frankenstein*, which takes a hard-headed look at the limitations of Prometheus and inspires similar enquiries in the speculative fiction that she initiates; and finally the experimental and political reperformances and reworkings of *Prometheus Bound* in the twentieth century, its continued use as a blazon of freedom, and the drift towards pessimistic readings. Common to these strands is a more or less explicit foregrounding of the nature and limitations of creative engagement with the ancient world, and who should do it.

Structure

For discussion of the main movements of the play, see especially Chapter 2, but for orientation I give an overview of the play. There are broad divisions between speech (in verse) and song (with 'recitative' somewhere in-between), but all action on the fifth-century stage is continuous. The labels parodos ('entrance-song'), episode (dialogue scene, not sung), stasimon (choral song) and exodos ('exit-song') do not seem to have been current at the time.[4]

1-127. Prologue
Hephaistos crucifies Prometheus under the direction of Kratos (Power) and Bia (Violence). Prometheus laments his fate in speech, recitative and song.

128-92 Parodos
Exchanges between the chorus (song) and Prometheus (recitative). The chorus enter in response to Prometheus' cries and question him about his fate.

193-396 First episode
In the first half (193-276), the chorus' questions prompt an account by Prometheus of the wars in heaven, Prometheus' support for Zeus and Zeus' harsh ingratitude. Prometheus tells of a card he holds against Zeus: knowledge of his downfall. In the second half (284-396) the chorus' father, Okeanos, flies in to sympathise and urge accommodation, but is rejected by Prometheus.

397-435 First stasimon
The chorus sing of how the furthest reaches of the human world, the world below and the rivers around it groan over Zeus' treatment of Prometheus.

436-525 Second episode
Prometheus' great speech on progress and civilisation (divided by four lines from the chorus), which sets out the skills that he has given mortals (deriving from the gift of fire).

526-60 Second stasimon
The chorus desire not to come into direct conflict with the overwhelming power of Zeus; they reiterate their sorrow for Prometheus but suggest his sympathy for humans goes too far.

561-886 Third episode
Enter Io, victim of Zeus' lust and Hera's vengeance. She has been half-transformed into a cow (retaining human form, but with horns) and is driven madly onwards by Hera's gadfly.

Prometheus relates Io's future travels and the end to her suffering. He consoles Io with the knowledge that Zeus is destined to fall, and that he will himself be released by Io's descendant (Herakles).

887-906 Third stasimon

The chorus sing of the benefits of marriage within one's station, not marrying the rich or the social elite; they deprecate entanglements with gods, drawing the lesson from Io.

907-1093 Fourth episode

Prometheus renews his defiance and elaborates the danger to Zeus. Hermes enters, to induce Prometheus to reveal the details. His threats to Prometheus become increasingly explicit: Zeus will send a thunderbolt and smash Prometheus underground for generations; when he emerges, generations later, Zeus' eagle will come and eat away at his liver. Prometheus remains defiant. The chorus decisively reject Hermes and remain loyal to Prometheus. The play closes with the storm raging about the Titan.

Date and authorship

Biographical and chronological information about ancient poets has to be treated with extreme caution, but Aeschylus seems to have started producing *c.* 500/499. It is probably true that he was born *c.* 525/4 in Eleusis to an aristocratic family, visited Sicily twice and died in 456 on his second visit. The charming detail that he was killed by an eagle dropping a tortoise on his bald head may not be reliable. The report of his fighting at Marathon, Salamis and Plataia is chronologically plausible.[5] Aeschylus' career thus covered almost the entire first half of the fifth century, although all his surviving plays date from the second half of his career: *Persians* (473/2), *Seven Against Thebes* (468/7) and *Suppliant Women* (probably 464/3) and the *Oresteia* trilogy (*Agamemnon*, *Libation Bearers* and *Eumenides*) of 459/8. Athenian tragedies were presented as part of a 'trilogy' or, strictly speaking, a tetralogy – a series of three tragedies, followed by (usually) a satyr play. *Seven* and *Suppliant Women* were each performed as part of a 'connected' trilogy, like the *Oresteia*, where the story continued across three plays. *Persians*, however, was part of an 'unconnected' trilogy' of self-contained plays, including a satyr play, *Prometheus*, usually identified with *Prometheus Pyrkaeus (Fire-lighter)*.[6]

The date and original context of the *Prometheus Bound* are, however, uncertain, and these are questions closely bound up with that of the authorship of the play. In some cases – as with the other six Aeschylean plays – a brief preface (*hypothesis*) derived from ancient scholarship may contain details of a play's original performance, including ancient disputes about authorship. Unfortunately, that of *Prometheus Bound*, like the majority of those of Sophokles and Euripides, lacks such information. This lack of knowledge is not itself unusual – only the discovery of a papyrus hypothesis to *Suppliant Women* located its Danaid trilogy after 469/8 (as it beat Sophokles who started in that year) and probably in 464/3, and thereby overturned many assumptions about Aeschylus' artistic development.[7] Ancient scholarship from the Hellenistic period onwards had no doubts about *Prometheus Bound*'s Aeschylean authorship. While this has some weight (they were entirely capable of disputing authorship, as with the *Women of Aitna* plays, or Euripides' *Rhesos*), this silence is not decisive.[8] Aristotle references a Prometheus play, probably meaning *Prometheus Bound*, in *Poetics*, but without indicating its author. Some of the vocabulary given to 'Aeschylus' in *Frogs* is suggestive of *Prometheus Bound*, but there is no direct quotation.[9]

Modern anxieties about the reliability of the ascription to Aeschylus stem from nineteenth-century scholarship, which, particularly in Germany, was keen to spot where plays had been modified or reworked by a later hand. Some such serious rewriting happened to the end of *Seven*, as we have it.[10] In the twentieth century, critics recognised that the oddities of *Prometheus Bound* could not be localised and introduced the idea that the play was not by Aeschylus at all ('spurious' in the critical jargon). Some of the less convincing doubts were raised because the play was felt to be philosophically, theologically or politically un-Aeschylean.[11] For a number of critics it is clearly a matter of taste, as some frankly acknowledge: for Martin West, the poet is 'brainless', the play 'inept', its morality 'shallow and trivial'; for Oliver Taplin, it is 'sluggish', 'episodic', 'grand and empty', and it is too political.[12] Even in less polemical studies, similar criticisms can be seen at work. The play certainly does not match Aristotelian precepts. There is a strong element of spectacle – which such critics wrongly downplay in Aeschylus – and there are some (exaggerated) difficulties of staging. The play also relies heavily on events outside the immediate time of the play and also on narration and confrontation – not unlike *Persians* or *Suppliant Women*, neither of which look Aristotelian. The nature and quality of the play's imagery has also been contested, but inconclusively.[13]

A better approach is to concentrate on stylistic differences between this and the other six surviving Aeschylean plays, where impressionistic 'feel' can be confirmed by statistical analysis. Such is (largely) the approach of Mark Griffith's exhaustive study, which sought to identify unconscious stylistic tics. The most significant of these are as follows. The play has considerably more speech and dialogue than song, the individual songs are less extensive, and the metres (rhythms) include types not used elsewhere in surviving Aeschylus (dactylo-epitrite, well-known from Stesikhoros and Pindar; and a form of 'enoplian'). Recitative anapaests less regularly have word-break (diaeresis) between them. The dialogue is less end-stopped, with sentences 'run-on' over the end of the line, reminiscent of Sophokles. The handling of the trimeter shares Aeschylean strictness, but with greater readiness to resolve the first anceps of the trimeter ('first foot anapaest'). Prometheus' opening speech, which shifts to recitative[14] to speech to solo song (monody) has no good parallel anywhere in Greek tragedy. There is a marked unconcern for hiatus between lines of dialogue ('interlinear hiatus'), which is unlike the other Aeschylean plays and both Euripides and Sophokles. *Prometheus Bound* is Aeschylean in its high style, a similarly low number of words to the line, a preference for compounds, and similar types of words being exploited, but it has a some-what more specialised vocabulary, uses some words that may reflect 'sophistic' influence and others where Aeschylus else-where prefers synonyms or near-synonyms. Elements of syntax are later than other Aeschylus.[15]

Prometheus Bound is thus Aeschylean in some respects, but diverges in others. Critics of such statistical analysis would suggest that with only six plays for comparison, three from the same trilogy, this is not a large enough sample to determine authorship with any confidence.[16] Other factors to consider include demonstrable variation in individual phenomena within other playwrights' oeuvres, where more plays or more widely distributed plays survive.[17] Within Aeschylus, other plays show outliers in certain phenomena, although none so consistently as *Prometheus Bound*. Some of these outliers may reflect artistic choice, particularly the more obvious lyric differ-ences, the treatment of speeches and actors' recitative.[18] Pinioning the central character for the duration of the play also affects other decisions concerning the play's form and structure.

If the peculiarities of *Prometheus Bound* are not put down to sample error, other explanations have been proposed. One has been to argue for a late development in Aeschylus' career, under the influence of early Sophokles, although the time for develop-ment between the *Oresteia* and Aeschylus' death is small. Another is to invoke Aeschylus' visits to Sicily.[19] More popular recently has been the suggestion that this was one of the four tetralogies of Aeschylus produced by his son Euphorion (Suda, *q.v.*), or that it was written by someone else in an Aeschylean manner. Philokles, his nephew, was particularly successful. Greek drama in the fifth and fourth centuries was very much a family affair and a number of sons produced their fathers' work pre- and post-humously (or were accused of doing so).[20] That the play is part-Aeschylean or pastiche Aeschylean is certainly attractive. The limitations of the statistical approach, however, mean that the case against Aeschylus is not absolutely conclu-sive, and for the purposes of this book I keep both options open.

Two closely related problems are the play's date and the

nature of its trilogy. *Prometheus Bound* was probably presented with *Prometheus Unbound* as part of a 'connected' trilogy. Scholia on *Prometheus Bound* 511 and 522 refer to *Prometheus Unbound* as 'the next play', and the most natural interpretation of this is that it refers to the trilogy sequence. The reference in the *Life of Aeschylus* to the 'Prometheus plays' (*Prométheis*) is also suggestive, albeit not decisive.[21]

In *Prometheus Unbound*, Herakles shoots the eagle torment-ing Prometheus and Prometheus is released (see Chapter 2). The main problem is identifying the other play, and whether it comes before *Prometheus Bound* or after *Prometheus Unbound*. The obvious candidate is *Prometheus Pyrphoros* (*Prometheus Fire-bearer*). Practically nothing survives and one of the two fragments seems to contradict *Prometheus Bound*: in the for-mer, Prometheus is to have been imprisoned for 30,000 years, in *Prometheus Bound* only for thirteen generations. Yet time is somewhat problematic in *Prometheus Bound*: Zeus is still a 'new' ruler at the beginning of the play, so there ought to be significant time lapse before the arrival of Io;[22] thirty thousand years is also a vague round number, like the ten thousand years suggested by Prometheus at *Prometheus Bound* 94, to which it is linked by an ancient commentator. The absence of evidence for *Prometheus Fire-bearer* is not uncommon, but some scholars suggest that this is the same play as *Prometheus Pyrkaeus* (*Prometheus Fire-lighter*) and the *Prometheus* satyr-play from 473/2.[23]

The possible story of a third play is also unclear. The amount of narrated back-story in *Prometheus Bound* makes an earlier play problematic, and if Prometheus is released in *Prometheus Unbound* and is reconciled with Zeus, the scope for a third play is reduced. If *Pyrphoros* is the missing play, then the title could allude either to the original theft of fire or to the ultimate institution of the Promethia in Athens, an aetiological conclu-sion akin to that of *Eumenides*. The latter seems to me preferable, but the identity of the third play may lie elsewhere, whether its title is preserved or not.[24] There is no convincing evidence for a connected 'dilogy' elsewhere and the Aeschylean colourings of *Prometheus Bound* would fit a characteristically connected Aeschylean trilogy, whether 'authentic' or not.[25]

The play has to be dated on the basis of its relationships to other texts, external allusions and formal criteria. The earliest references to the play are in Aristophanes' *Knights* (425/4), which parodies two lines from *Prometheus Bound*,[26] and more substantially in *Birds* (415/4). These need not imply that the tragedy was recent: compare Euripides' *Telephos* (439/8) parodied in *Akharnians* (426/5) and *Thesmophoriazousai* (412/1); Aeschylean plays also seem to have been reperformed by 425.[27] A slightly earlier date can be established by a parody of *Prometheus Unbound* by Kratinos' *Wealth Gods* (see Chapter 2), fairly securely dated to 430/29. The upper limit is established by a reference in 351-72 to the eruption of Mt. Aitna, in Sicily, in 479 or *c.* 475, also alluded to by Pindar, *Pythian* 1.15-28.[28] There are also strong echoes of Aeschylus' *Suppliant Women*, particularly in the figure of Io. Together, these data indicate a date between 463 and 430. The lack of securely dated Athenian literature between 458 and 430 makes more precision unwise, and other allusions are less clear cut.[29]

Some of the staging techniques (Chapter 4) suggest a late or post-Aeschylean date. There is no unequivocal evidence for a stage-building (*skênê*; not known before the *Oresteia*), but its presence would resolve some of the staging problems. It seems overwhelmingly likely that the crane (*mêkhanê*) was used, which itself probably requires the *skênê* as cover; the crane is in use by at least 432/1. The play also uses three speaking parts in its opening scene; again, no play before the *Oresteia* (and the spurious end of *Seven*) requires more than two. The sources are hazy, but indicate that the third actor was added towards the end of Aeschylus' career.[30] Although form and stagecraft seem to have developed in non-linear fashion, a date late in Aeschylus' career (if Aeschylean) or in the decade or two afterwards, seems likely.[31]

Two important areas of interpretation are affected by the date. Firstly, the internal and external political context changed considerably between 463 and 430. The account of freedom, tyranny and progress will look very different against that changed background. Secondly, the relationship of *Prometheus Bound* to the rapidly developing intellectual culture of Greece is contingent upon the date. Some scholars regard an Aeschylean *Prometheus Bound* as too early for its use of 'sophistic' language and ideas and so either deny the influence or deny the date but I argue in chapter 3 neither position can hold, particularly if plays engage in political and intellectual debate rather than simply responding to it.

Historical and political context

The context for *Prometheus Bound* is thus either (if Aeschylean) the years immediately before or after the reforms of Ephialtes (462/1), which seem in some form to have removed the remnants of traditional power structures and checks upon the Athenian democracy; or (if post-Aeschylean) during the highpoint of the radical democracy that emerged in the two and a half decades before the Peloponnesian War, a period associated with the pre-eminence of Perikles. That the play belongs to the period when Athens' democracy was at its most energetic and ambitious is surely not coincidental. What is, perhaps, hidden in such an assessment is the degree of political and ideological controversy throughout both periods.[32]

Athenian democracy was barely forty years old by the mid-460s, but had already evolved after the original reforms of Kleisthenes in 508/7. Traditional centres of power were eroded, particularly the annual magistrates (arkhons) and the old aristocratic council, the Areopagus, which was composed of ex-arkhons. The introduction of a board of ten generals elected on a tribal basis (501/0) led to the displacement of the traditional war-arkhon (*polemarkhos*) and opened up one route to power. This displacement was, at least according to Herodotos, evident at Marathon (490) and certainly seems to have been complete by the time of the Persian invasion (481-79).[33] After Marathon, the arkhons were weakened by the introduction of an element of the lot into their selection procedure (487/6). It is likely that there would have been some (long-term) knock-on effects on the composition and authority of the Areopagus.[34] Politics was, however, still dependent at this point on the big man, particularly from one of the traditional families; the introduction of ostracism (first used in 488/7) served as a counterweight to the possibility of one man becoming too powerful.[35]

Following the defeat of the Persian invasion, Sparta walked away from active leadership of the Greek states. Athens, who had close links with the island states and some of the cities of Asia Minor, took the leading role in what became the Delian League. The League consolidated control in the Aegean and scored a series of further successes against the Persians, culminating in the battle of Eurymedon (probably 469). In this aggressive posture, Kimon, son of Miltiades was the key player. Although nominally still allied with Sparta, Athens was developing a hegemonic naval power which might threaten Sparta as the traditional leader of Greece. As long as Kimon's star was undimmed, the external and internal position was sustainable. Kimon was opposed to radical change and was a particular friend of Sparta.[36] Within Athens, dispute centred on the controversial figure of Themistokles, who may have represented more democratic opinion (he is associated with Ephialtes in a chronologically confused section of *Ath. Pol.*), but was ostracised in the late 470s or early 460s.[37]

Both the incipient international rivalry and domestic tensions at home came to a head in the late 460s, as events played into the hands of Kimon's enemies. First, in late 466/5 (or 465/4), Thasos sought to secede from the Delian League, which led to a lengthy campaign and siege to bring it back to the fold, not completed until 463/2. Shortly after Thasos revolted, an attempt to establish a colony at 'Nine Ways', in Thrace, met with disaster and a massacre at Drabeskos (465/4). Both the absence of Kimon and the failures in the North Aegean seem to have provided an opportunity for radical democrats led by Ephialtes. Ephialtes undermined the power of the Areopagus through a series of prosecutions, including (unsuccessfully) one of Kimon on his return.[38] Meanwhile, Sparta, ravaged by an earthquake (*c.* 465), faced a revolt by its helots (serf class) and called in the Athenians to help put it down. Kimon led Athenian troops to Sparta. In his absence, Ephialtes, in 462/1, passed legislation to hobble the Areopagus constitutionally and hand its constitutional powers to democratic institutions. The precise nature of these reforms is debated, but probably encompassed the transference of powers of scrutiny of office-holders (*dokimasia, euthynai*) and perhaps forms of initiating prosecutions in relation to major offences against the state (*eisangelia*).[39] Henceforth, the Areopagus would be a murder court alone. Then, the Spartans, who had grown concerned about the Athenian presence on their soil, worried that the democratic soldiery would side with the revolting helots, sent the expedition home. The democrats exploited this opportunity to shift Athenian foreign policy by tearing up the alliance with Sparta, and initiating an alliance with its traditional Peloponnesian rival, Argos.

This period was the most serious internal political crisis between 507 and 411. Kimon, on his return from Sparta, tried to reverse the reforms of Ephialtes and was ostracised (462/1). Ephialtes was assassinated, a rare political murder in Athens before the late fifth century.[40] As hostilities opened with Sparta and her allies, the opening stages of the so-called First Peloponnesian War, rumours of fifth columns and betrayals by the Kimonian faction swirled.[41]

This is the background for the *Oresteia*, which enacts a progression from the pursuit of justice by vendetta through to the institution of trials, with the Areopagus the foundational court. The final play, *Eumenides*, establishes the mythical basis for both the internal reforms and the new foreign policy. Such an implicit endorsement of the new order is tempered with calls for stability and consensus, calls which were much needed.[42] If *Suppliant Women* is 464/3, then its presentation of a pointedly democratic Argos is more plainly an act of political provocation, but like the *Oresteia* it is not simplistic.[43] If *Prometheus Bound* is by Aeschylus, its enactment of another kind of social and political progress would have been part of the same context, whether during the height of the reforms or in the febrile atmosphere afterwards.

Following the break with Sparta, Athenian ambitions become markedly more pronounced. Further political reforms followed: opening up the arkhonship and thus the Areopagus to the zeugite (hoplite) class (457/6), introduction of local courts (453/2) and the citizenship law (451/0) which established national identity (Athenian parentage on both sides) as a criterion for privilege, regardless of class. Introduction of jury pay probably dates to this period. Perikles, probably part of the Ephialtic circle, was the prime mover in at least the last two.[44]

The 450s see Athens attempt to develop a hegemony on land. After initial success, particularly in relation to Megara and a partial set-back at Tanagra (?457), Athens established control of Boiotia at the battle of Oinophyta and also disposed of a longstanding local naval rival, the island of Aigina. By the 440s, this effort collapsed, after Boiotia successfully revolted (447/6) and Euboia shortly afterwards, before being reconquered. A peace treaty with Sparta ('The Thirty Years Peace') was signed in 446/5. Athenian efforts in central Greece were muted thereafter.

Wider geopolitical ambitions also increased. An expedition to Egypt in the late 460s or early 450s, in support of a revolt against Persia, met with initial success but was countered by Persian forces and the expeditionary force was trapped and destroyed (*c.* 455 or *c.* 458/7[45]). This experience put an end for a few decades to the wilder shores of Athenian expansionism. Consolidation of the Eastern Mediterranean included repeated operations in Cyprus, with a final return to action for Kimon. A notional or perhaps formal peace with Persia existed after 449, with the Delian League in control of the Eastern Mediterranean and Persian activity focused on local subversion rather than military confrontation.

The League was clearly no alliance of equals, with many allies preferring to pay money for protection rather than contribute ships and men. With the move of the League treasury from Delos to Athens (454), the League is effectively an Athenian empire. In 440 (early summer 441/0), one of the still-autonomous allies, Samos, revolted, and Perikles led the campaign to restore Samos to the League and establish democratic government, not completed until the following year. Tensions with Sparta increased throughout the 430s, leading to the outbreak of war in 431. The entire post-Ephialtic period is often known as Periklean Athens, but his pre-eminence really dates from the Samos episode and his chief political opponent, Thucydides son of Melesias, was ostracised in 444/3. If *Prometheus Bound* is post-Aeschylean, then it could be at any point in these developments.

The Athenocentric view is not the only one to consider, however. Aeschylus was evidently interested in Sicily, where the cities in the east and north of the island were major Greek centres throughout the first half of the fifth century, initially under powerful tyrants, such as Gelon and Hieron of Gela and Syracuse, who defeated a major Carthaginian force in 480; by the mid-460s they had given way to constitutional and democratic government.[46] On his earlier visit, Aeschylus wrote his *Women of Aitna* for Hieron for the founding of his city of Aitna. Sicilian references in *Prometheus Bound* do not, however, mean that the play was written for performance there any more than Egyptian references in *Prometheus Bound* or *Suppliant Women* indicate an Egyptian performance,[47] but they certainly show the extent to which Athens is plugged into a broader Mediterranean political and cultural environment, and that the trials of Athenian democracy are taking place within and against both a cultural interest in that environment and a foreign policy context in which the growing democracy has increasing ambitions.

Overall, whether the play is by Aeschylus, a revised version of an Aeschylean model, or post-Aeschylean pastiche, its central themes of tyranny and rebellion, materialism, technological progress and cultural optimism, and a self-conscious approach to spectacle and political grandstanding are all particularly pointed in the years around and following the reforms of Ephialtes and the final moves towards a radical democracy.

Narrowing that context further may not, on current evidence, be possible, but I will be considering in subsequent chapters the possible historical implications of the Promethean provocations and challenges within these chronological parameters.

2

Gods and Other Monsters

The principal narrative strand of *Prometheus Bound* is concerned with tyranny and rebellion. The context is one of faction fighting amongst the gods, and the long and bitter struggle for divine supremacy. The presentation (and critique) of the gods and the presentation of autocratic rule – monarchy or tyranny – address questions of legitimacy and the relationship between ruler and ruled. For many subsequent writers, these were the dominant elements of the play. For the republican Milton, the issue of divine monarchy and the challenge to it formed a central tension within his later epic and dramatic works. For the Romantics, issues of freedom and revolution took a much more explicitly sceptical turn. Both in their different ways were concerned to reflect on how the Promethean activist could be reflected in the human agent, how to move from the divine to the human level. This allegorical question is the major challenge of *Prometheus Bound*.

Succession and authority

The play opens with Prometheus brought out to a remote spot in Skythia (1-2, 21-2) by two heavies, Kratos (Power) and Bia (Violence), and tortured. Kratos menaces and intimidates another participant, the god Hephaistos, who reluctantly wields the implements. Hephaistos offers sympathy for the plight of the victim, but acquiesces in nailing him to a crag, in a form of crucifixion. He is not only fixed there to suffer exposure, constrained position, and sleep deprivation (32), but is actually impaled onto the rock (64). Such punishments were, in the

Greek world, the privilege of traitors or the lowest sort of criminals.[1] As a god, the punishment could be eternal. Who is this rebel, Prometheus? Just what has he done to deserve this?

The back-story of *Prometheus Bound* adapts the works of the early Greek poet Hesiod: *Theogony*, which details the struggle for succession between generations of gods, and *Works and Days*, which explains the place of humans in the current order. *Prometheus Bound* alters the place and nature of humanity and modifies Prometheus' role, but the background of divine infighting remains much the same, predicated on a logic of serial patricide.

At the start of the play, Zeus has only just acquired the reins of power and withstood attempts to displace him. The dynastic struggle is well into its third generation. The primeval regime of Ouranos (Heaven) is overthrown by his son Kronos (by Gaia, Earth). Kronos castrates his father, which enables his fellow-gods to be born (*Theogony* 147-210). Kronos is often accounted the ruler of a golden age (cf. *Works and Days* 109-19). He in turn attempts to thwart the ambitions of his children (by the goddess Rhea), and swallows them at birth. Zeus, however, avoids becoming dessert. Advised by Ouranos and Gaia, Rhea replaces the infant god with a stone (*Theogony* 453-500). Zeus grows up to take revenge on his father, forces him to vomit up stone and siblings, and takes over the family business.

The new regime faces two significant crises. Firstly, Zeus is challenged by gods of his father's generation (and their descendants), the Titans. The Titanomachy (war against the Titans) involved all the children of Kronos on Zeus' side and was said to have lasted for ten years (*Theogony* 636). Like other major mythological wars – the Gigantomachy (gods against giants), Centauromachy (Lapiths against centaurs) and Amazonomachy (Greeks vs. Amazons), the Titanomachy in part dramatises an opposition of order or culture against chaos or nature. The forces of order, however, only survive through the crudest of tactics. Zeus calls up from Tartaros (the lowest part of the underworld) the 'Hundred-handers', the last-born children of Ouranos and Gaia, imprisoned by Zeus at the start of his reign, but called upon for this exercise of power politics (*Theogony* 617-731).

A second challenge is an even more monstrous figure – Typhoeus (or Typhos or Typhon) – the final spontaneously-born son of Gaia. Zeus again resorts to brute force: his thunderbolt (820-80). For Pindar (*Pythian* 1.16-28), this victory represents the triumph of harmony, justly wedded to power. But there is a disturbing edge: the Cyclopes, yet another set of the monstrous offspring of Gaia and Ouranos released from captivity, build these smart weapons for Zeus (*Theogony* 501-6).

In *Prometheus Bound*, the back-story is revealed slowly over the course of the play, as the captive Prometheus discusses his situation with a series of arrivals, each of whom has their own relationship to him and the current power. These encounters provide a filter through which to view this larger conflict and substantially rewrite the mythological past. In the Hesiodic account, Prometheus is a second-generation Titan, the most prominent of the offspring of Iapetos, all of whom were punished by Zeus for acts of rebellion. These included Menoitios and Atlas (destined to carry the world on his shoulders) as well as Prometheus' foolish twin, Epimetheus.

Prometheus, for Hesiod, is the arch-trickster who even tried to outsmart Zeus and is thus responsible for the parlous state of humanity, the removal of fire, which he steals back, and the invention of Pandora, the first woman, and her jar of troubles (see further Chapter 3). In *Prometheus Bound*, however, Prometheus is not compromised as he is in Hesiod, even if still a canny operator. The source for his exploits is Prometheus himself, but he is not contradicted by any of his interlocutors on the basic facts. In the Titanomachy he tried to persuade his fellow Titans not to attempt to overthrow Zeus by violence, but to use wily schemes (*haimylas mêkhanas*, 206) and cunning (*dolos*, 213). When the Titans decided to press ahead with violent regime change, Prometheus switched sides (216-18) and advised Zeus on how to overcome Kronos and his fellow Titans. Prometheus' cunning has not been directed wilfully at Zeus.

Another important shift is that when Prometheus changed sides, he brought his mother with him. She is no longer Klymene, a daughter of Okeanos (*Theogony* 508), but Themis (18), who is further identified with Gaia (Earth). In a pointed passage (209-10), Prometheus explains the identification. He is thus now Zeus' uncle, a first-generation Titan, not his cousin.

Themis was usually a distinct goddess, who personified order and legitimacy. Her role implies that Zeus needs to acquire legitimacy and that Prometheus himself is bound up with its delivery. Moreover, Themis is a source of both prophecy (211) – linked to Prometheus' foresight – and good sense. Themis is described by Hephaistos as *orthoboulos* (18), literally 'giving straight advice', which connotes both legality and plain-speaking. This echoes the important, if enigmatic, role of Gaia in Hesiod as dispenser of tactical advice.

Now, however, Prometheus has fallen out with the new ruler. The reason is that he took pity on mankind and came to their aid, when Zeus was about to sweep them away. The reasons for Zeus' hostility are not explained, beyond their association with the old regime. Prometheus stole fire to bring succour to humanity. Zeus' response is this brutal, personal punishment.

A question that may occur at this point is why Prometheus has not simply been blasted by the thunderbolt, like his brother Titans. The answer is twofold, practical and political. As Prometheus reveals progressively over the course of the play, in particular to the chorus and to Io, he has a hold over Zeus: he knows his future. The succession wars are potentially not over. There is a prophecy that a child will be born mightier than the father. In Hesiod's version, Zeus avoids such conception by swallowing his bride, Metis (Craftiness). Their daughter, Athena, thus sprang fully-formed from Zeus' head (*Theogony* 886-900, 924-6). In other versions, as in *Prometheus Bound*, the mother is Thetis, who is ultimately married off to a mortal, Peleus, instead. Pindar's account (*Isthmian* 8.26-52; ?478 BCE) has Themis playing the central prophetic role. In another version, the child stronger than Zeus is Typhon/Typhoeus himself (in the *Homeric Hymn to*

Apollo 326-74). This is the version developed by Shelley in *Prometheus Unbound*.

There is, then, a double rebellion by Prometheus: helping mortal men and refusing to reveal the future. Although the treatment of Prometheus is set up as a punishment, it is also a form of torture, to encourage Prometheus to talk. The gradual release of the back-story intensifies the confrontation with the absent Zeus, who works through proxies. Zeus' stance has turned an ally into a serious threat.

There is, however, a further reason for Zeus resorting to torture rather than the thunderbolt. Just as the unfortunate experiences of the twentieth century have shown, in such regimes as Pinochet's Chile, Pol Pot's Cambodia or Mugabe's Zimbabwe, torture is not only a method of extracting information (unreliably) from victims, but also a way of attacking and breaking resistance and opposition to a regime. Prometheus is being punished in order that he might recant his opposition to Zeus and thereby serve as an example and a warning to others. As Kratos puts it, punishment is only one step in Prometheus' re-education (*Prometheus Bound* 8-11):

> For such a crime, I tell you,
> he must pay the penalty to the gods,
> so that he may learn to love Zeus' regime
> and cease his human-loving ways.

Like Winston Smith in George Orwell's *Nineteen Eighty-Four*, Prometheus has to learn to love Big Brother – or, as in this case, Big Nephew.[2]

Tyranny and resistance

Prometheus Bound is in the first place, then, a study of the nature and application of power. The series of characters with whom Prometheus interacts flesh out the operations of autocracy, in a series of cameos displaying different responses to the establishment and maintenance of power through brute force and intimidation. It is repeatedly emphasised that Zeus is but lately come to the throne, and in the most violent of circumstances. The play presents an all too familiar narrative of violent repression following a *coup d'état* and the installation of a new dictator.

In his splendid isolation, Prometheus is perhaps the most compelling of those subjects, but his interlocutors are also highly significant, both for defining the central figure and for exemplifying victims, collaborators or representatives of the regime. Already in the opening scene (1-127), compare the enthusiastic sadism of Kratos with the queasy response of the god-technician Hephaistos.

As abstractions associated with Zeus, Kratos and Bia derive from Hesiod (*Theogony* 385), as part of a group of personified concepts with very little development. In *Prometheus Bound*, they embody the new regime. Through Kratos in particular, the power of Zeus is elaborated as one of physical violence and crude intolerance. Kratos' mouth is as ugly as his appearance (78); he refers to his own impatience and harshness (79-80). Like Zeus, he is *trakhys* (rough and ugly, 80, cf. 35, 186). Kratos repeatedly emphasises the need for Hephaistos to be more violent than necessary (*biai*, 74; cf. 15, 52, 55, 58). Kratos may be drawn with a very broad brush, but he represents the kind of uncomplicated thug for whom despotic regimes offer countless job opportunities. But he also has a set of principles: pity is a waste of time, pointless, irrelevant (36, 43-4) – at least, pity for one's enemies (36; also 67-8). Kratos embodies retribution. The rule of law is the rule of fear (41). Both he and Hephaistos acknowledge Zeus as hard and oppressive (*barys*, 'heavy', 77, cf. 17).

Kratos' notion of justice (*dikê*, 30, cf. 9), which Prometheus has transgressed, is one of cosmic hierarchy: he has given divine privileges (*geras*, 38; *gera*, 82) to mortals. The term is often used of sacrificial gifts, but here evokes aristocratic notions of social and political value. The breach of the social divide constitutes an act of violation (*hybrize* 82). Although such allocation often requires social consent, it should be Zeus, the monarch, who allocates privilege.[3] Kratos makes the further striking proposition that under the monarchy, no-one is truly free – and Hephaistos agrees (49-51):

Krat.   Everything is a burden, except lording it over gods:
        for there is no-one who is free except Zeus.
Heph.   I know it, from this evidence, and I can say nothing
        to refute it.

The use of *eleutheros* (free) situates the play within fifth-century debates over the nature of political rights and freedoms.[4] Life under Zeus is one of constant surveillance (53-4). Is it possible to be free under such rule? Not for Kratos or Hephaistos.

Hephaistos has a more complex emotional response. He has form as a divine victim (*Iliad* 1.571-600), but being directed and bullied by a personified abstraction is a new low. He admits the force of Zeus' command (12-13, cf. 3), but wishes that someone else had been assigned the task (48). He expressly does not want to carry it out (19) and suggests it goes too far. The job requires 'boldness' (*tolma*, 14-16), which connotes recklessness and risk. He uses the term of Kratos and suggests that it correlates with a lack of pity (42). Against Kratos' emphasis on (hierarchical) family loyalty and obedience, Hephaistos sets friendship and family solidarity (39). Even so, Hephaistos also suggests that Prometheus' actions edge from bravery to bravado: certainly, he argues that cowering before the other gods is reasonable (29-30). The main note, however, is one of sympathy. He dwells at length on the future suffering of Prometheus (20-34) and repeatedly stresses his sorrow, despite the taunting of Kratos (66, 69).

Most striking is Hephaistos' lament over his technical skills that have put him in this position (45), which sets up an ongoing debate on the social and political function of technology. Hephaistos faces a moral choice about its use in inflicting pain (acknowledging that Prometheus would have a legitimate complaint, e.g. 63). For Kratos, technology is morally neutral – responsibility lies with the wielder (46-7). Despite anxieties over Prometheus' cunning (in escapology, 59), he maintains the technology of pain and physical repression against Prometheus' skill (83-7) and all-encompassing means of finding a way (cf. 111). The relationship between material and political *tekhnê* is clearly being posed (62):

> ... he shall learn, even if he is a skilful operator (*sophistês*), that he is slower than Zeus.

Zeus has used his own skill and that of his pain-technicians to pin down Prometheus. Whether this is the definitive exercise of *tekhnê* will be a question addressed in the play. Zeus is implacable and 'difficult to influence' (*dysparaitêtoi*, 34), but this will be a battle of skill and, indeed, principle, as well as of wills.

The word used by Kratos for Zeus' regime is *tyrannis*. The modern association of tyranny with despotism and repression does not necessarily hold for Archaic Greece, but by the mid-fifth century in Athens, such associations could be exploited. Plays of the period, such as Sophokles' *Ajax* (*c.* 450) and *Antigone* (*c.* 442) present the *tyrannos* in those terms, as ruling without consent, using violence and threats, and implicated in financial corruption.[5] In Aeschylus, there are plays where the term is clearly avoided, as in *Persians* or *Suppliant Women* (with its highly democratic monarchy); in the *Oresteia*, the term is ambivalent, but is used of the usurping Klytaimestra and Aigisthos in a plainly negative fashion.[6] *Prometheus Bound* likewise exploits the negative connotations.

Authoritarianism is associated with such a regime. 'Whoever has newly come to power is harsh' (35), says Hephaistos.[7] The theme is explored further as Kratos, Bia and Hephaistos leave. Prometheus' first speech starts by reflecting on his torment, leading to a denunciation in anapaests of his treatment by the new chief of the gods, using a term, *tagos* (96) with military connotations, again associated with tyranny.[8] He recovers himself, however, and briefly sets out the theft of fire and its benefits for mortals. He claims to know the future and to have steeled (or resigned himself) to it, but also knows that it will not be forever, as Hephaistos has already hinted, perhaps unwittingly (101-3; cf. 26-7). He is, however, startled by a noise and fears the worst, breaking into startled song and back to more measured trepidation as to what will happen.

In contrast to Kratos, Bia and Hephaistos, the chorus of daughters of Okeanos arrive with altruistic motives and an independence of spirit. They have heard the hammering and come to investigate. As the daughters of the god who represents the ocean that encircles the world, they are close to *Prometheus Bound*'s remote location. The shocking sound has disrupted conventional patterns of behaviour (their *aidôs*, respect or sense of shame, 134) and they have argued their father around to let them leave their home (130-1). Their opening words, 'Do not be afraid: it is in friendship that this formation ... has come' (128-30) develop the sympathy of Hephaistos' remarks, but in much less cowed fashion. They develop the idea of Zeus – and indeed the Olympians as a group – as authoritarian ruler (149-51):

> For new helmsmen
> are masters of Olympos,
> and it is with new laws
> that Zeus is ruling without legitimate authority,
> and he is annulling the previous mighty regime.

The political language is unambiguous: the new generation of gods are 'helmsmen' (*oiakonomoi*, 149), using the common ship of state metaphor, as extensively in *Seven*.[9] Zeus invents laws without due authority or legitimacy (*athetôs*[10]) Later, Prometheus describes Zeus as a *prytanis*, the term for a member of the executive committee of the Athenian council (169).

The chorus develop the characterisation of Zeus and his subjects. They reject the idea that a god could be unsympathetic or (worse) take pleasure in Prometheus' fate – except, that is, Zeus (160-2; sentiments repeated at 243-5). The evidence belies this (Kratos and Bia), but it is important that for the chorus sympathy is normative. Zeus is so extreme in his oppression of the gods (164-5) that they can only envisage Zeus either having his fill of violent pleasure or being removed in a coup. This sets up Prometheus' revelation of his trump card. The future (beyond *Prometheus Bound*) hinges upon how Zeus deals with this possibility. Prometheus looks ahead to a day when Zeus will soften (188) and readily (if not necessarily willingly) accept Prometheus as a friend (191-2). Prometheus' comment that Zeus keeps justice (*to dikaion*) close to himself indicates that justice is personal: this may change.

The chorus' sympathy is not without significant reservations. Just as a 'bold-hearted' god enjoys pain (160), so too Prometheus is bold (*thrasys*, 178) and not prepared to slacken sail in a storm. Picking up Kratos and Hephaistos' discussions of freedom (*eleutheria*), they describe Prometheus as 'speaking with excessive freedom' (*agan eleutherostomeis*, 180). The question raised, regardless of context, is whether Prometheus is too much the rebel.

The first episode falls into two parts: in the first, Prometheus explains the situation and back-story. The chorus, tellingly, invite Prometheus to speak 'if it does not hurt you to talk' (196). Prometheus presents the war in heaven as *stasis*, the civil conflict that blighted Greek cities in the fifth century, particularly in the conflict between democratic and oligarchic factions.[11] The Titans, who refused to listen to him, thought they could, like Zeus, 'gain mastery by force' (*pros bian ... desposein*, 208). Prometheus sets his persuasion and ideas against violence, but perhaps disingenuously: his ideas seem to encompass the invention of the thunderbolt, which sends Kronos and his allies (221) down to Hades. Prometheus emphasises the mutual nature of his decision to stand by Zeus (*hekonth' hekonti ... xymparastatein*, 218). Zeus, however, has violated this mutuality (224-5):

For there is this sort of sickness in a tyranny
not to trust one's friends.

The breakdown derives from Zeus' intention to annihilate the human race and create a new one (232-3), again reworking

Hesiod. Prometheus explains that he saved mankind by providing both hope and technology, symbolised by and originating in fire (234-54); see, further, Chapter 3. Just as Hephaistos and the chorus show pity for him, Prometheus showed pity for the human race (238-46). Zeus denies pity to both.

The chorus seek to clarify why Zeus responded quite so violently. Preventing annihilation in itself, they think, would not have been enough. 'You didn't, I suppose, go even further than this at all?' (247), the chorus leader tentatively asks. When he tells them the full story, the chorus are shocked (259-62):

> How will he decide that? What hope is there? Don't you
>   see that
> you made a mistake? In saying that you made a mistake
> there is no pleasure for me, and for you there is pain. But
> let's drop this, and you look for some kind of release
>   from your ordeal.

Prometheus snaps a response: it's easy for the free to give advice to prisoners. Prometheus claims that he foresaw that he would be punished and willingly took on the task – again the point of will (*hekôn hekonta*) is stressed – although he did not think the punishment would be so severe. As well as prickliness, there is uncertainty in his foresight and a neediness in urging the chorus to listen (274) and in his appeal to solidarity (275), to which the chorus assent.

The entrance of their father, Okeanos, who flies in to offer sympathy and assistance, initiates the second half of the episode. Okeanos is both Prometheus' half-brother (through Gaia, 301-2) and his father-in-law (555-60). He is self-important, long-winded, pompous (288-97) and somewhat humorous. Prometheus expresses surprise at him showing such nerve (*etolmêsas*, 299) and scepticism about his intentions (303). His complaints to Okeanos echo those earlier in the scene, focusing on Zeus' treatment of a friend and ally (304-5). Okeanos' response urges Prometheus to be pragmatic (307-10):

> I see you Prometheus, and it is advice I want to give you
> as to the best course of action – although you are a
>   cunning devil.
> Recognise who you are and adapt your ways
> to the new order: for there is a new ruler (*tyrannos*) too
>   among the gods.

Okeanos goes further than his daughters in arguing for political pragmatism. The language of the new ruler and the best course of action picks up both Prometheus' account of his advice to the Titans (204) and the chorus' earlier attempts to reason with Prometheus (316, cf. 262). Okeanos advises Prometheus against speaking angrily and describes Prometheus in terms reminiscent of the characterisation of Kratos and Zeus earlier (*trakheis* 311, cf. 35, 80, 186; *orgê*, anger, 315, cf. 80), which Okeanos likewise uses of Zeus (324).

Okeanos suggests that Prometheus is too mouthy (318-19, 327-9), because of pride in his intellect. Okeanos presciently observes that this will only make things worse: it will make his current sufferings 'a joke' (314). Picking up the language of restraint from Kratos, he utters some chilling advice (322-4):

> So, if you use me as a teacher,
> you will not kick your leg out against the goads, seeing
>   that
> there is a prickly monarch in power and one not subject
>   to scrutiny.

The political language is unmistakable. Scrutiny is central to the ideology of the radical democracy and was undoubtedly central to the Ephialtic movement; here it is counterposed to monarchy and tyranny, the same opposition played out in Herodotos' 'debate on the constitutions' (3.80-3). Equality of speech (*isêgoria*) is also prominent in Herodotos' accounts of early democracy (5.78.1). Okeanos' advocacy of politic quietism – *hêsykhia* to its advocates (cf. 327), *apragmosynê* to its critics – is antithetical to democratic ideology as articulated in Perikles' funeral speech (Thucydides 2.35-46), but advocated by conservatives as in Pindar, *Pythian* 8.1-20 (446 BCE).[12] Okeanos' self-conscious apology for offering 'old advice' (*arkhaia* 317) has political overtones.

Resistance to such a tyrant, Okeanos advises, is useless (329). His offer of mediation (325-6, 335-9) meets with sarcasm about playing both sides (330-1), faint praise for his keenness to help (340-1), scepticism about Zeus' openness to persuasion (333) and advice to stay out of the way (334, 344-6). Prometheus throws both futility (*matên*, 341) and quietude (*hêsykhaze*, 344) back at him. Prometheus recalls others persecuted by Zeus: Atlas (347-50) and Typhos (351-72). Atlas, as Prometheus' (and Okeanos') brother, evokes the family dimension to the divine struggle.[13] Prometheus' account of Typhos' attempt to dethrone Zeus (357) likens rebel and persecutor: the assault and the defeat are through pure violence (*bia*, 353, 357). Typhos lies trapped under Mt. Aitna, barbequed by Zeus' thunderbolt, spewing forth flames in his fury (*kholos*, 370), the very term used by Prometheus in describing Zeus' present attitude (376). Typhos blasted out of his 'pompous arrogance' (360-1) recalls the warnings Okeanos addressed to Prometheus earlier (318-19) but with two distinctions: Prometheus is offering resistance but not violence (cf. 380); and Prometheus has a plan.

Prometheus' attitude towards Okeanos, despite exaggerated courtesy about his political sophistication (373-4), is haughty, not dissimilar to Antigone's rejection of Ismene (*Antigone* 536-60). The frostiness comes to a head as Okeanos persists with the possibility of interceding, and Prometheus rejects assistance. Each asserts his good intentions and sense (385-6). Prometheus accuses Okeanos of stupidity and warns against pushing Zeus into hostility. This warning is hardly sympathetic: Okeanos is still trimming, despite his claim to being willing to be bold (381). Prometheus' caricature of Okeanos' intervention as a 'lament for me' (388) is sarcastic; Okeanos returns the sarcasm in suggesting that Prometheus will learn from his own experience – a common Aeschylean motif.[14] This is capped by Prometheus' final dismissal: 'go, ride, keep your current good sense' (392).

Okeanos huffily replies that he was going anyway – his steed is keen to be home. He flies off.

The heart of the play swings the focus back onto humanity. The chorus sing (first stasimon, 397-435) of their weeping for Prometheus and Zeus' violence against the other gods, ruling as a law unto himself (*idiois nomois kratynôn*, 403-4). The whole world, physical and above all human (406-24), is in sympathy with – struggling with (*synkamnousi*, 414) – the trials of Prometheus' family.[15] Prometheus then gives his great speech outlining the benefits that he has given mortals. The following dialogue with the chorus reveals that Zeus is subject to fate: the great leader is not the helmsman (*oiakostrophos*, 515, cf. 149), but the fates are: his rule will end. The chorus' response is to express fear of Zeus and their trembling at Prometheus' punishment, but they also question Prometheus' commitment to mortals: the favour cannot be returned nor help repaid. Mortals, they argue, are weak and transient; they are also disruptive of Zeus' order (*harmonia*, 547-51). Whereas Okeanos had suggested that Prometheus is too proud, they argue that Prometheus cares too much for mortals: in a striking reversal, he has too much *reverence* for mortals (543).

At this point, there is a really surprising entrance: Io, the daughter of Inakhos. A relatively restrained anapaestic segment and astrophic song is followed by a wild exchange with Prometheus, with her singing in dochmiacs. She has been transformed partially into a cow (horned, 588) and driven out of Argos, a punishment from Hera for becoming the object of Zeus' lust. Hera set Argos, with his countless eyes, to watch her, but he was killed by Hermes on Zeus' orders. In retribution, Io has been sent mad, wandering the world. Traditionally, she is spurred by a gadfly, which she describes early in her solo song, but in terms as much mental as physical. The ghost of the dead Argos pursues her.[16] Sounds and images terrify her.

Io is a formal and thematic double of Prometheus. Her entrance, recitative and monody, recalls Prometheus' lament in the prologue. Both blame Zeus for their sufferings. Prometheus alludes to Hera's role (592), but Io blames Zeus (577-81):

Whatever, son of Kronos, whatever was it that you
    found me guilty of
that made you yoke me in these pains,
ai, ai,
and made you lacerate me like this with gadfly-driven
    fear,
terrified, out of my mind?[17]

Io is another victim of violence (*pros bian*, 592). Similar language
describes their afflictions: harnessing and taming, hunting, and
storm imagery.[18] The principal differences are that Io is (part-)hu-
man and her torture is one of constant movement, Prometheus'
that of immobility and refusal to submit. After the chorus' preced-
ing song, Io appears the exemplary victim, standing for the whole
human race, at the mercy of Zeus' capricious power. Just as Zeus
was bent on wiping out the human race, so too Io's expulsion from
her home by her father was a direct and unwilling (*akousan akôn*,
671) consequence of Zeus' *bia* (672), his threat to wipe out another
genos (667-8, echoing 232-3). Zeus' sexual tyranny and violence
(736-41) stands for his broader political tyranny.

    Io's account of her experiences and Prometheus' account of
her future travel all further this impression. There is, however,
more to Io than exemplary victimhood. She is not too absorbed
in her misfortunes to show sympathy for Prometheus, as from
her entrance (561-4) – until the madness overwhelms her. Pleas
to reveal her future are intertwined with requests for information about Prometheus' plight (613-14, 617-20). Prometheus'
attitude here differs markedly from that towards Okeanos. The
wish to spare Io from harm appears more sincere, tinged with
palpable sympathy (624-30, 636-9) and invoking friendship
(611). There is a community of suffering and mutual sympathy.
Despite their reservations, the chorus are important in developing this idea in their response (687-95) to Io's sufferings. It is
they who prevail (698-9, 782-5, 819-22) upon Prometheus to
reveal fully Io's future.

    Io's distressed response to Prometheus' revelation of her
travels from Europe to Asia (700-41) leads to important plot

developments, as they explore their mutual hatred of Zeus. Prometheus discloses how Zeus' tyranny will end (755-75), through the 'empty-minded schemes' (*kenophronôn bouleumatôn*, 762) of his sexual adventures. Prometheus reveals that a sexual target will give birth to a son more powerful than the father (768) and only Prometheus can prevent it, if released (769-70). It will be one of her descendants, thirteen generations hence, who will release him. Zeus' sexual adventures thus create the conditions both for regime-change and Prometheus' own release. Prometheus' further narratives relate Io's travels across Asia down into Egypt (787-818) and, with a digression on her past experiences to prove his reliability, the Egyptian end-game and her descendants, including the daughters of Danaos that will take the family line back to Argos. Her descendant Herakles, the 'famous archer' (872) is not named, but unmistakable.

As Io departs, the chorus reflect upon the dangers of tangling in marriage with the powerful. They desire never to attract Zeus' wandering eye and fear they could never escape his cunning (*mêtis*). In the final episode, Prometheus elaborates Zeus' downfall. His description of his future son echoes both Hesiod's Typhoeus and the Typhos under Mt. Aitna. The chorus suggest Zeus can never be mastered (930) and caution Prometheus again about speaking too openly. Prometheus, however, is supremely disdainful as he was earlier of Okeanos (937, cf. 392), and affects unconcern. The chorus, unlike their father, stick around. Their sympathy and fear, despite Prometheus' hauteur, is central to the final scene, as Hermes arrives (941) to extract the details of Zeus' fate (947-8).

Hermes is the most sophisticated of Prometheus' opponents, subtler than Kratos or Hephaistos, sharper than the self-advertised teacher of good sense, Okeanos. The confrontation fizzes as Hermes addresses his response to power, and questions his actions. Hermes, for Prometheus, is 'the new tyrant's flunkey' (942); Prometheus, for Hermes, is an arrogant, self-willed *sophistês* (a clever-dick: see Chapter 3), a prideful boaster (944, 947). The *authadia* ('wilfulness') of which Prometheus accuses

2. Gods and Other Monsters

Zeus (907; cf. Kratos at 79) is turned back at him by Hermes (*authadismasin*, 964; cf. 1012, 1034, 1037; Prometheus' denial at 436); likewise, Prometheus' pointed claim to Io that it is right to speak plainly to friends (609-11), and his insistence throughout on frank speech, meet with an invitation to speak plainly about Zeus (949-52). There are insults and threats, but also clever attempts to provoke Prometheus into answering. Hermes plays on Prometheus' pride: the political player reduced to impotence (966-9):

Prom. I would not exchange my misfortune –
       know it well – for your servitude.
Herm. Right: it's better to be enslaved to this rock
       than to be a faithful messenger for father Zeus.

In a jagged but accelerating exchange of stichomythia, Hermes accuses the Titan of glorying in his predicament, of offering childish insults, lacking sense (*sôphrosynê*), being mad and going against paternal authority. Prometheus comes back on these with some grandstanding positions, but by no means caps Hermes' remarks. Hermes' opening moves are mostly psychological – the physical threat is veiled, but none the less effective. The sequence of one- or two-line exchanges is broken by a cry of pain from the Titan which Hermes interrupts: 'Zeus does not know this expression' (980). The change of speaker mid-line, unusual for Aeschylus and *Prometheus Bound*, accentuates Hermes' subtle brutality.[19] Bravado from Prometheus foregrounds the physical punishment. Hermes responds with more cutting remarks about the efficacy of such bravado (997); in a cute approach to Prometheus' daring, he suggests that Prometheus has not been audacious enough (999-1000):

Dare, you fool, just dare one time
to think straight in response to your sufferings.

Prometheus dismisses capitulation as 'begging like a woman' (1005) and now Hermes takes the gloves off. Prometheus' pointless sophistication (1011) and wilfulness (1012-13, 1034-5) are

41

addressed with the language of horse-breaking: Prometheus to be tamed, Zeus the civilising force. Hermes lays out the future: Prometheus' burial in Tartaros as Zeus blasts his crag and his re-emergence to have his liver eternally pecked out. This prophecy, says Hermes, contrasting his own and Prometheus' promises, is no empty boast (1030-1). The chorus intervene, urging Prometheus to moderate his stubbornness and listen to Hermes; Prometheus continues in his defiance (1040-53). Hermes washes his hands of the Titan and turns to the chorus, advising them to leave before the cataclysm comes (1058-62), but the chorus refuse, despite the reservations they have expressed and Prometheus' sometimes cruel words. They prize loyalty and solidarity most of all (1068-70):

> For I have learnt to hate traitors,
> and there is no disease
> which I spit out more than this.

The final confrontation, then, does not involve Prometheus, for all his magnificent defiance, but the chorus and Hermes. Hermes departs with a parting shot that they should not complain if they bring disaster on themselves out of stupidity (*hup' anoias*, 1079). Their decision is not explicable to Hermes. The chorus are not exceptionally bold, self-willed, defiant, knowledgeable or powerful, yet they choose to stay. This decision has troubled some critics, but it is the culmination of a pattern of behaviour which is at the heart of the play.

Unlike many Aeschylean (or Sophoklean) choruses, the chorus of *Prometheus Bound* do not offer abstract reflections around the themes of the play; nor do they sing great hymns, which would be signally inappropriate here; rather, they respond directly, emotionally and personally to the events that they witness. This has been characterised (inaccurately) as weak, simplistic and un-Aeschylean,[20] but their personal and complex response is central to the play's political concerns. The chorus are terrified, but nonetheless they stand up to their father to see Prometheus and to Prometheus where they think him unreasonable. Despite their reservations over his stubbornness and assistance to humanity (allayed in the Io scene), they are prepared to risk Zeus' wrath to stay with their friend. Prometheus has the grand speeches of defiance, the contemporary political language, and a stratagem in reserve with which to confront the terrifying power of Zeus; the chorus have none of those things, but they have the crucial element of sympathy. Mutual solidarity is the core of their resistance to power.

From divine to human

This discussion of the divine politics of *Prometheus Bound* may obscure just how odd it is to have a Greek tragedy performed on the divine level at all. Within the world of the play, the human race's survival and the nature of its society are at stake, but humanity itself has only Io as a representative on display. This is unlike most tragedies and ancient scholarship noted it as a peculiarity of Aeschylus and older tragedy. The Prometheus plays are given as examples.[21] In surviving tragedies of Sophokles and Euripides, the role of the gods as active participants on stage is usually highly circumscribed, limited to the prologue or a final appearance to resolve a crisis (the so-called *deus ex machina*[22]); even in Euripides' *Bakkhai*, the human dimension is central. Even for Aeschylus, *Prometheus Bound* takes this emphasis on the divine plane to an extreme; not only are Olympians and Titans involved, but personified abstractions – even rarer on the tragic stage.[23]

This mode of presentation poses challenges for relating divine and human concerns.[24] This has most often been posed in theological terms, as an assault on the Olympians or religion in general. On the most literal reading, however, the gods remain a disagreeable fact of life. Their behaviour is at issue, not their existence (975-6):

To put it plainly, I hate all the gods:
all the ones that are happy and treat me abominably,
    without justice.

The nature of the gods proposed by *Prometheus Bound* has been objectionable to many classical critics, as it has been persuasive to radicals: their dissociation from justice, *dikê*, and association with crude politics.

Part of the problem is that in the nineteenth and early twentieth centuries, Aeschylus was interpreted as a profound theological thinker, presenting in his plays a quasi-monotheistic 'Zeus-religion', intimately related to justice, *dikê*. The *Oresteia*, in particular, presented a temporal and spiritual progression from blood-feud to constitutional justice, guaranteed by the new order of Zeus. Nothing, it seemed, could be further from the image of Zeus in *Prometheus Bound*. A consistent theological perspective could only be achieved by denying Aeschylean authorship, rereading *Prometheus Bound* as an endorsement of Zeus, or positing a similar theological and moral progression in the Prometheus trilogy.

The view that Aeschylus was creating a monotheistic theology or that his Zeus differed substantially from the inherited one was comprehensively demolished by Lloyd-Jones.[25] He went further, however, and denied any progression in either the Prometheus trilogy or *Oresteia*: Zeus and the Erinyes make a deal, they do not change character – and likewise Zeus in *Prometheus Unbound*. This goes too far. In the *Oresteia*, Zeus clearly changes his stance. There is, however, little *theologically* that hangs upon it. There is aetiology (explanation) of contemporary religious practice and there is serious religious poetry, but the progression is on the human level, the morals and politics that Zeus guarantees.[26] *Prometheus Bound* and the Prometheus trilogy are somewhat different.

Violence and capriciousness are embedded in the Greek concept of the divine, from Homer onwards (e.g. *Iliad* 1.560-600), and even when the other gods contest Zeus' will there is acknowledgement of his supreme power, as at the death of Sarpedon (16.431-61), although there are other emotions on display there beyond Zeus' anger.[27] Zeus' violent aspect is even stronger in Hesiod's *Theogony*, both in the wars of succession and his serial rapes. There is, however, a broad movement from monstrosity in the earlier generations to civilisation and order, embodied by Zeus and the Olympians. It is a harsh justice, however: in the original Hesiodic account, Prometheus may never have been released – that element entered the Hesiodic tradition later.[28] In *Works and Days*, Zeus is more explicitly presented as a guarantor of justice and punisher of transgressors. Zeus' ultimate guarantee of a Greek victory at Troy is similar: the conflict stemmed from a breach of hospitality, over which Zeus stands guarantor.

In Aeschylus there are broadly similar assumptions about Zeus, as guarantor of order and justice, and a subtle god. This is particularly true of *Suppliant Women*. The chorus of Danaids, fleeing from marriage with their cousins in Egypt, enter with an invocation of Zeus (especially 86-95) and return to him throughout the play, as god of suppliants and hospitality, and their ancestor, through Io.[29] Zeus, for the suppliants, is bound up with *dikê* (590-9); as the Argive king notes, he regulates society through force and fear (478-9, cf. 615-20).

In the *Oresteia*, however, the handling of Zeus and *dikê* clearly develops. There are parallels with the *Suppliant Women* in the first play, *Agamemnon*, with Zeus linked to justice and guarantor of hospitality (*Agamemnon* 60-1). As the trilogy progresses, conflicting interests develop about the nature of justice. Reciprocal justice is initially associated with Zeus, but subsequently justice becomes more nuanced. To avenge Agamemnon, Orestes kills his own mother, Klytaimestra, and her lover, Aigisthos, in *Libation Bearers* explicitly on Apollo's orders (especially 899-902). The Olympian then seeks to uphold the legality of this killing in the final play, *Eumenides*, which provides an aetiology for legal process in general (associated with Zeus), and its specific manifestation in Athens. *Eumenides* also provides an aetiology for the social order, patriarchy, as Athena subordinates the claims of Klytaimestra and the Erinyes in Zeus' name (734-43, 794-9).[30]

In its handling of the divine, *Eumenides* is the closest surviving Aeschylean tragedy to *Prometheus Bound*: the conflict between the deities is the centre of the play. The complaints of the 'old' gods, the Erinyes, at their treatment in the hands of the new order (640-3, 778-93) are similar to those of Prometheus' account of the new gods in *Prometheus Bound*. Athena, however, despite embodying force, also exercises persuasion (881-91) to integrate the Erinyes into the new order, offering reformulated privileges as well as implied threat. There is thus (reluctant) social and political consensus, as well as legal and social order. This entails some development on the part of the gods, but the focus is on their guarantee of the human order rather than their own character.

Any association of Zeus with reason, order and justice is, however, flagrantly challenged in *Prometheus Bound*. Zeus' justice is personal and capricious (186-7, cf. 149-52). Despite Hermes' articulation of patriarchal order at the close, the regime is rooted in violence and intimidation, both towards gods and men. The political language is far stronger than in *Eumenides*, even though the latter is founding an Athenian institution. To see Zeus as anything other than a tyrant, in the fullest sense, is doomed.[31]

Paradoxically, the location of *Prometheus Bound* on the divine plane undermines any sense of a conventional religious element. In the *Oresteia* the hymns and laments of the humans in *Agamemnon* and *Libation Bearers* express their experiences of and anxieties over the divine, and provide a rich context of religious belief and practice against which the cosmic drama of *Eumenides* is played out. *Prometheus Bound* shows less direct human experience of the divine, and necessarily not in its choral parts. As for Zeus, he has to move at least some distance in *Prometheus Unbound* to save his skin. The implications of the change for the divine or human order depends upon whether *Prometheus Bound* is part of a trilogy and how that trilogy plays out.

Reconciliation or victory?

Viewed as a single play, *Prometheus Bound* ends on a note of defiance and solidarity. The audience knows that Prometheus will be released centuries later, that Herakles shoots the eagle, that Zeus is not overthrown and that Thetis is married off to Peleus. How Prometheus gives up his secret and how Zeus relents is unclear. Will Prometheus triumph and Zeus fold? Will there be a mutual unbending of stiff necks? An ending this open can have its own sort of narrative satisfaction, but it is rather alien to Greek tragedy and suggests that there will be continuance in *Prometheus Unbound*. As both Zeus and humanity survive, there will be movement – on both parts.

The fragments of *Prometheus Unbound* offer the following sequence of events, again (excepting Herakles) on the divine plane. Like *Suppliant Women*, the play opened with a choral entry (fr. 190). The chorus are Titans, Prometheus' siblings, released from captivity in Tartaros.[32] In recitative anapaests, possibly in an exchange with Prometheus,[33] they describe their search for their brother, their wanderings throughout the world, from the very south (fr. 192) to the boundary between Europe and Asia (fr. 191).[34] In probably the first episode, there is a long speech from Prometheus which, as in *Prometheus Bound*, sets out the back-story, recounting his punishment by Zeus and the attentions of the eagle. He describes the gnawing of his liver and its regrowth. Substantial parts of this are preserved in a translation by Cicero (*Tusculan Disputations* 2.23-5 = *Prometheus Unbound* fr. 193). Prometheus' defiance is signally muted (fr. 193.22-8):

> Thus I have lost control even of myself: I endure these
>   trying afflictions
> desiring death in the search for an end to my misery.
> But I am pushed far from death by the power of Zeus,
> and this long-lasting wound, heaped up in the dreadful
>   centuries,
> a device of torture, has been planted in this body of
>   mine,
> from which drops of blood, melted in the sun's warmth,
>   drip,
> which stain continually the rocks of the Caucasus.

The nature of the subsequent action is unclear. The play featured an encounter with Herakles, journeying into the north and west on his quest for the cattle of Geryones (fr. XIII G), and perhaps also the apples of the Hesperides, via his brother Atlas.[35] Prometheus relates to Herakles, in an echo of the Io scene, the peoples and places he will encounter en route (frr. XI-XIV G). Herakles at some point shoots the eagle (fr. IX G).[36] *Prometheus Bound* 771 suggests that the initiative was Herakles', in a spontaneous act of human kindness, although he did not go further out of fear of Zeus (Servius on Vergil, *Eclogues* 6.42 = fr. XVc G). Zeus may have acquiesced (cf. Hesiod, *Theogony* 527-9), particularly now that Prometheus' stubbornness has been worn down, or this may have been part of a deal between Prometheus and Zeus. More likely is that the rapprochement follows the shooting. The act of kindness by a descendant of Zeus (fr. 201) following Prometheus' physical battering may have facilitated that deal.

Zeus' pursuit of Thetis has begun by the time of *Prometheus Unbound* and brings him nearby.[37] Whether he, she or both appear on stage is unclear. An appearance by Thetis would echo Io (as victim of Zeus) and (as daughter of Okeanos) the chorus of *Prometheus Bound*. An appearance by Zeus would be unusual for tragedy, although not for comedy (to which the encounter between Prometheus and Zeus in Lucian's *Dialogues of the Gods* may owe something).[38] Rather, Prometheus' route to Zeus is likely to have been through a proxy, as in *Prometheus Bound*. The hypothesis to *Prometheus Bound* erroneously lists Ge (Gaia, Earth), Prometheus' mother, with Herakles in the cast of *Prometheus Bound*; she, like Herakles, may be a prime mover in *Prometheus Unbound*. None of the fragments confirm this, but she probably appears on a vase clearly inspired by *Prometheus Unbound* (see further Chapter 4). Prometheus' access to his piece of knowledge about Zeus' future is because of Ge/Themis. Perhaps through Ge, Prometheus reveals the threat that Thetis poses to Zeus and as a result (fr. XVa G) is released.[39]

The precise terms of the reconciliation remain uncertain. Explanations of two Greek practices may be involved: wearing garlands (fr. XVIa G = Athenaeus 15.674d), as compensation (*antipoina*) for Prometheus, and wearing rings of stone and iron, explained as a symbol variously of victory or incomplete or only provisional release.[40] All these require some movement by Zeus, just as he has already moved in releasing the Titans.

There are hints of some underlying themes, particularly relating to humankind, in fragments that belong to Herakles' journeys. The peoples that he is to visit include both some that are fierce and warlike (the Ligurians, fr. 199) and others that are peaceful and just. The latter encompass versions of the people that Zeus turns to in the *Iliad* 13.1-6, when he is tired of the fighting. The Gabioi (Homer's Abioi) seem close in some respects to Hesiod's golden race – they live the life of justice, *dikê* and the earth produces food of its own accord (fr. 196). Addressing the state of mankind, most of whom are not living such a life, may be central to the final resolution of the divine conflict in the trilogy. If so, the Prometheus trilogy, like the *Oresteia* may be providing an aetiology for what constitutes *dikê* for humanity, guaranteed both by Prometheus' philanthropy and Zeus' acquiescence.[41] Other elements that have been linked to the denouement include the story of Kheiron taking the place of Prometheus, alluded to at 1026-9, and an aetiology for the Athenian festival of the Promethia, which included torch races. Notwithstanding the element of aetiology in *Prometheus Unbound*, there is certainly scope for development in a further play, whether *Fire-bearer* or another.[42]

Audience, identity and political allegory

The conduct of *Prometheus Bound* and *Prometheus Unbound* on the divine plane not only raises religious issues, but also poses in sharp form a problem of engagement common to Greek tragedy. Given the distance in time, space and class, how does an audience relate emotionally and cognitively to tragic characters and situations? The play certainly has much to say about humanity, not least in Prometheus' great central speech and its framing choruses. and their very existence is the root of the dispute between Prometheus and Zeus. The bulk of the action of the play, however, and its emotional and political content are in the first instance about relationships between gods. The most straightforward human point of contact is Io. Unlike the bulk of the Athenian audience, she is female, royal and part-cow. As so often in Greek tragedy, audience engagement is with the other. The interplay of distancing and engagement is the essence of Greek tragedy. The distancing allows for a reflective dimension, for abstraction and generalising; sympathetic understanding of characters allows for application to their personal circumstances. Both forces are at work in *Prometheus Bound*.

Among the elements that facilitate such an interplay in *Prometheus Bound* are anthropomorphism and personification, so important in Greek thought. The gods can come close to abstract forces, as in Hesiod's *Works and Days*, beyond the mythological opening. Elsewhere, however, from the *Iliad* onwards, the Olympians behave in ways that are recognisably human, albeit with much more dangerous consequences: lust, revenge, pride, hurt, and shame are only some of those qualities. It is thus possible to understand (and sympathise with) such characters. It is not, however, just the Olympians to whom human characteristics can be attributed. Abstract concepts can themselves be thought of as agents and in human terms. The genealogies of the gods in Hesiod's *Theogony* offer striking examples, as well-known gods and monsters with associated mythological narratives give birth to a series of personified abstractions. The anthropomorphised Kratos and Bia of *Prometheus Bound* represent abstract ideas made concrete and (particularly Kratos) understandable through their actions and character. These personifications thus use human understanding in order to explore the abstract and the general and relate it to material consequences. Likewise the Olympians and Titans are themselves bound up with abstract concepts, as with Zeus and *dikê*/Dike.

Whatever the appropriate language might be for a Greek god, the starkly political and intellectual language used in *Prometheus Bound* is not it. This is, rather, creative anachronism.[43] The juxtaposition plays off familiar (abstract) language against the remote made concrete and enacted on stage, which might be viewed as a kind of Brechtian alienation effect, distancing the audience and forcing them to reflect on the socio-political dimension of both the play and themselves. The inconsistency is, however, consistently inconsistent: a fantastic and anachronistic environment is created, rather than an unsupportable contradiction.

The distancing is most pronounced with Prometheus and with his off-stage antagonist, Zeus. Prometheus, to be sure, is working (he claims) for human interests. He is *philanthrôpon* (28). His qualities of pride and anguish are certainly recognisable. But the scope, scale and consequences of his actions are beyond the human scale. His punishment, certainly, evokes an Athenian one, but is exaggerated, even without the supplement of burial alive followed by the eagle. The tenor of his resistance, too, is superhuman. He is an amplification of the elite individuals at the heart of most tragedy: comparison has often been made with the grand individualists of Sophokles' tragedies, such as Antigone and Ajax.[44] Even so, if Zeus and Prometheus do ultimately bend their stiff necks, there is enough in their characterisation to offer some example to humans, just like the far more alien Erinyes in the *Oresteia*. Far less exemplary or admirable, but more recognisably human are Okeanos or Hermes, who offer a means of exploring possible reactions to a political situation.

Still closer to the human audience, and arguably even closer than the part-human Io, is the chorus of Okeanids, notwithstanding that their perspective on the human race is a major contribution to the play. Three elements create an impression of humanity. Firstly, they are far more concerned about social convention than the other characters – such as their persuasion of their father. Secondly they are far more conscious of their vulnerability than any of the other gods, even than Okeanos, and are ready to express fear for themselves both as a collective and as individuals. Thirdly, they do not have the monomaniacal consistency or stubbornness of a Prometheus or Zeus. They

51

change their mind rapidly in response to ongoing developments. Nothing could be more human.

Human vulnerability is a feature in many choruses of Greek tragedy, who frequently represent the vulnerable or marginal, such as women or slaves, contrasted with the audience, who are broadly, and certainly ideologically, citizen males.[45] The presentation of otherness facilitates exploration of the emotional dimension of the story. In political terms, the relations between characters are central: the chorus afford one way of demonstrating the effect of rulers' decisions on the ruled. As a collective, any chorus invites identification from the audience, the principal collective within the theatre, but they are by no means an 'ideal' internal audience. The chorus' advice to Prometheus is hardly consistent, let alone authoritative.[46] Positive positions emerge from the interplay between Prometheus and the chorus, Prometheus and Io, and to a lesser extent Prometheus and Okeanos, and they centre on sympathy and solidarity as principles of action. A diverse range of characters – god and human, male and female, individual and collective – from their different perspectives and identities converge upon the same point.

The Athenian politics of *Prometheus Bound*

Care, then, is taken to relate the divine politics to human politics, to emphasise that this is about politics and power, not about theology in the first instance. The interplay of universal and concrete that marks *Prometheus Bound*, as most tragedies, provides for cross-cultural understanding, but it would also have specific resonances in Athenian culture.

The first filter is tyranny as seen within democratic Athens. *Prometheus Bound* was produced two generations after the historical tyranny of the Peisistratids and at least one since tyranny was an actual threat: the Persian expedition to Marathon, accompanied by the returning Hippias, and the wave of ostracisms in the 480s. Conceptually, however, tyranny continued to be the position against which the Athenians identified politically.[47] By the 420s, at least, tyranny could be attached to any potential disruptive political elements, individuals or groups: even as early as the 440s, it could be used for oligarchic groups and conspiracies.[48]

The tyrannicides Harmodios and Aristogeiton were celebrated, however inaccurately, as heroes (or foundational war-dead) of the democracy in popular song, public ritual and most conspicuously by statues placed in the Athenian agora – and pointedly replaced after the first group were looted by the Persians in 480.[49] They embodied democracy's self-definition against tyranny and the application of traditional aristocratic notions of *philia* (friendship) in its service.

Tyranny within Athenian democracy represents a concern about internal threats, not only force – although fifth-century Greece is replete with examples of internal *stasis* (often combined with external threats) – but also populism, which is intrinsic to Greek tyranny. Any sufficiently dominant, successful and powerful politician could become associated with the concept. Some specific historical frames are possibly relevant to *Prometheus Bound*.

Firstly, some echoes of politics in Aeschylus' plays may suggest Themistokles. Although much of his career after the Persian War is poorly-attested, he was clearly cautious towards Sparta, was instrumental in the rebuilding of Athens' walls despite Spartan unhappiness and prevented retaliation against Argos, traditional enemy of Sparta, for staying out of the fighting against Persia. Themistokles was ostracised in the late 470s, whereupon he took initial residence up in Argos and travelled the Peloponnese, plausibly to stir up trouble against Sparta. Sparta sent an embassy to Athens with alleged proof of conspiring with the Persians (medising), as a result of which he was condemned in his absence and hunted by a joint Spartan and Athenian team. Escaping via Corcyra and northern Greece, he fled to Asia Minor (*c.* 465 or later) and ended up in Persian service. One scenario is that he fell victim to the growing influence of Kimon. The beginning of the 460s mark the high-point of Kimon's ascendancy, and the disappearance and arguably persecution of this famously wily and forethinking

(Thucydides 1.138) representative of the earlier generation of political leaders may find an echo in *Prometheus Bound*.[50]

How close Kimon's leadership style was to the autocratic Zeus is difficult to determine, but Zeus' treatment of a one-time political rival has some congruence. Conversely, the reaction against Kimon in the 460s brings in additional resonances, less as a direct allegory (although the potential fall of Zeus may offer some purchase) than in terms of the ideological conflict of the time between an extension of democratic principles and the facilitation of persistent dominance by a narrow elite. Prometheus' extension of privilege to mortals finds an echo in the Ephialtic movement that sought to open up centres of aristocratic power and displace the person most associated with that constitutional arrangement.

Other possibilities arise, if *Prometheus Bound* is post-Aeschylean. There are well-attested allegories between Olympians and Athenian politicians by the 430s but quite possibly earlier: with Perikles and his associates. The period of his unbroken run of generalships (*stratêgia*) was characterised in the sympathetic account of Thucydides as 'in name a democracy, but in practice the rule of the first citizen' (2.65.9); he is echoing the abuse of Perikles as Zeus and/or a tyrant in the comic poets – both may indicate wider popular use of the analogy. It is much harder to see a direct parallel for Prometheus, but the points made about the extension of privilege versus narrow domination again find echoes.[51]

That the Athenians *could* interpret the story of Prometheus and Zeus in such political terms is indicated by the earliest reception of *Prometheus Unbound* in Kratinos' *Wealth Gods* (*Ploutoi*), whose parodos clearly parodies that of the tragedy. The eponymous Wealth Gods of Kratinos are also Titans, associated with wealth through a reference back to Hesiod's myth of ages. They have come looking for another Titan, their brother (*Wealth Gods*, fr. 171.121-5):

As the rule of tyranny has ended
and the people are in power (*dêmos ... kratei*)

we have rushed here to look for our kin
our old brother
looking for him even if he is by now decrepit.

Binding and theft are both mentioned (fr.171.16, 21). The reference to the tyranny and the *dêmos* are usually understood as using the familiar Zeus/tyrant/Perikles link in comedy and alluding to the fining of Perikles and the abrupt ending of his continuous *stratêgia*.[52] If so, a date of 429 is suggested. The play evidently blended together a mythological frame with a contemporary political frame – the trial of Hagnon, an Athenian general with Periklean links, apparently for some form of financial corruption.[53]

The allegorical moves of comedy are blatant.[54] This contrasts with the more restrained, consistent and logically coherent approach of Greek tragedy. Consequently, the kind of political parallels that I have been drawing in this last section are somewhat unfashionable, the sort of approach often derided by literary critics as the mistreatment of tragedy by historians. To make Greek tragedy meaningful, however, an audience will always be relating the events on stage to their own personal knowledge, circumstances and experiences. Meaning and interpretation always requires some kind of allegorical move. While the problems of dating *Prometheus Bound* mean that there are a number of possibilities, exploring these kinds of comparisons is essential to understanding Greek tragedy in its historical context.

Summary

In *Prometheus Bound*, then, the account of divine succession and a broad movement towards *dikê* is thoroughly rewritten. Zeus' representation as a capricious tyrant represents the gods in a far more explicitly political vein than is usual, and the exploration of the rift between Prometheus and Zeus sets up an investigation of the nature of power and of different responses to it. The unusual setting on the divine plane is an extreme instance of tragic defamiliarisation, but also introduces per-sonification and allegory to explore abstract concepts, while also tying the action back to the human scale through the language of contemporary politics. Points of identification for a human audience are less with Prometheus himself than with the chorus of Okeanids and with the (part-)human Io, but they share with the Titan, and to a lesser extent Hephaistos and Okeanos, the quality of sympathy, which is presented as central to personal and political relationships. This does not exclude more specific allegories that the audience may wish to draw with their political context, then or, indeed, now.

3

Technology and Civilisation

In addition to the highly politicised and authoritarian representation of divine order, the second intellectual challenge of
Prometheus Bound is its account of human civilisation. In contrast to the profoundly pessimistic view of human culture inherited from archaic Greece, *Prometheus Bound* articulates an
optimistic, progressive vision of human self-reliance and self-
sufficiency, rooted in technological progress, permeated with
the language of a growing Greek materialism, relativism and
scepticism. Whereas in some hands the combination can lead to
a toxic reactionary philosophy, *Prometheus Bound* seems to be
crystallising the embryonic stages of radical democratic theory.
There is a strong hint, however, that materialism by itself is not
enough, but the gap is to be filled with politics and civil society,
not with religion.

As with the discussion of tyranny in the previous chapter, the
analysis I give here stands at odds with accounts of Greek
tragedy that have sought to divorce it from its political context
in general or its democratic context in particular, or to distin-
guish tragic universalising from political intervention.[1] It also
disputes the claim of some historians that there was an absence
of democratic theory, whether that is ascribed to the hazards of
preservation or to Athenian democracy being driven by practice
rather than ideas.[2] The origins of Athenian democracy may
indeed have been somewhat haphazard or accidental, but by the
middle of the fifth century, matters are much more ideological
and focused. It is not a coincidence that it was in the period of
the Ephialtic reforms and their aftermath, that Aeschylean
tragedy is exploring the authority of the people (*Suppliant*

Women) and articulating one sort of progress (*Oresteia*). *Prometheus Bound* takes these ideas much further and provides a universalising rationale for progress and participation, as well as freedom – all cornerstones of radical democracy and particularly meaningful at that time.[3]

From pessimism to hope

Early Greek thought was dominated by the idea of decline from a more fortunate, even idyllic state of the world. This 'lapsarian' ideology (i.e. oriented around the fall of mankind) dominates the epic tradition, in both its 'heroic' and 'didactic' forms. The warlords (*hêrôes*) in Homer's *Iliad* are said to be stronger than men of the narrator's own time, and themselves lesser men, physically and morally than their ancestors. As Nestor, the man with the longest memory at Troy, says (*Iliad* 1.259-72[4]):

> But listen: you are both younger than me.
> For once before now I associated with men
> even better than you, and they never disregarded me.
> I had never yet seen such men, nor shall I see
> men like Peirithous and Dryas, the shepherd of his
>   people
> and Kaineus and Exadios and godlike Polyphemos
> … no one would match them
> of those who are now mortal men upon the earth.

The same backwards-looking perspective is shared by Hesiod, who begins his advice on farming and associated matters with two related stories which explain the present state of the world – full of misery, pain and hard labour. One is the story of successive races (golden through bronze and iron; *Works and Days* 106-26) and the other is the myth of Prometheus and Pandora (*Works and Days* 42-105). There are ways of reconciling the two stories, but they are best understood as parallel aetiologies (explanations) of physical, economic and moral decline (and have obvious parallels with the Judaeo-Christian

Fall). The golden race of men belonged to the time of Kronos, and enjoyed land that produced food spontaneously, without labour. The succeeding series of men were progressively less just, especially in relations with the gods, and endured more hardship, symbolised by their eponymous metal. The race of heroes interrupts this progression, but the current race, the race of iron, are beset both by labour and by the flouting of justice (*dikê*).

In the case of the Prometheus and Pandora narrative, man earlier had to work for only one day a year. The blame for the fall from this state of affairs is laid squarely at the feet of Prometheus (*Works and Days* 47-58):

> But Zeus was angry in his heart and hid [man's
>   livelihood]
> because crooked-thinking Prometheus had deceived
>   him;
> for this reason, then, he devised grievous troubles for
>   mortals,
> and he hid fire; this in turn the noble son of Iapetos
> stole for mortals from cunning Zeus
> in a hollow fennel-stalk, evading Zeus who delights in
>   thunder.
> Zeus who gathers clouds was angry and addressed him:
> 'Son of Iapetos, cunning above all others,
> you delight in your theft of fire and deceit of my wits,
> a great source of pain to you yourself and to men of the
>   future.
> I will give an evil to them in return for the fire, in which
>   all
> will delight, embracing harm to themselves in their
>   hearts.'

Zeus initially hides man's livelihood in response to the swindle that Prometheus engineered in the division of portions in sacrifice, a story retailed at length in the *Theogony* (521-616, especially 535-561). The attempted trick, in which humanity is complicit, makes their fall self-inflicted, a loss of *dikê*, but the story is not quite consistent with the account of the golden race, in that spontaneous production does not figure in this pre-lapsarian world. Rather, fire is introduced as a gloss on *bios* (livelihood), suggesting cooking and baking in particular, and fire it is that Prometheus steals back. This association of fire with human livelihood is developed in *Prometheus Bound* well beyond what is only implicit in Hesiod.

Zeus escalates the conflict and creates his ultimate weapon – Pandora and her jar of mischief. Pandora is sent as a bride for Prometheus' foolish brother Epimetheus, who has hindsight (*epi-*) rather than foresight (*pro-*). Epimetheus (*Works and Days* 83-9, *Theogony* 511-14) accepts Pandora as a gift from Zeus; she opens the jar and lets out pain, misery and disease into the world. Pandora here stands as the first woman. Epimetheus, like his brother, is represented as close to man. Woman is thus a punishment for man, although facilitated by male stupidity – both themes developed at length by Hesiod. This gendering of the human condition is not so obvious in *Prometheus Bound*.

The only possible consolation in Hesiod is that when the bad things fly out of Pandora's box, one element is left, hope, which is stuck under the lip of the jar (*Works and Days* 94-100). This may mean that it remains under human control, but the image is somewhat ambiguous – it could imply that hope did not escape into the world: the ambiguity is not irrelevant to Hesiod's presentation which maintains a belief in the association of Zeus with *dikê*, but is nonetheless pessimistic about the state of the world and the possibility of alleviating it.[5] Hope becomes an important part of the Prometheus myth in many of its post-Aeschylean guises. Indeed, it might also be said to be the kernel of progressive utopian thought.[6]

The lapsarian trend died hard in Greek thought. Notwithstanding increased material wealth and gradual social and political reform, the dominant perspective is backwards looking. Even advocates of (moderate) political and social reform such as Solon downplay the aspiration and are anxious about unrestrained hope.[7] It was not until the fifth century that accelerating speculation about the material nature of the world, increased interest in the nature and limits of human thought and human society, and rapid political and social change led to accounts of technical and social progress, accounts to which *Prometheus Bound* looks and arguably contributes.

As with the wars of succession, Hesiod's account of humanity is thoroughly rewritten. There is no attempted trickery at Prometheus' behest, no falling from *dikê*. Rather, in the aftermath of the succession battles, Zeus has allotted realms and privileges (*gera*) to the various gods, but has no place for humans. Instead, he intends to dispose of them altogether (229-36) and replace them with a newer model. This decision certainly evokes the Hesiodic myth of races, but in *Prometheus Bound* the current human race is the original and only human race: there is no sequence of material and moral decline, so much as a cataclysmic 'Year Zero'. The association of the original human race with the time of Kronos seems to be the problem. The threat to humanity echoes the chorus' description of Zeus' attempt to wipe out the works of the earlier gods (*aistôsas* 232, cf. 151).

Prometheus' response to Zeus' genocide is revealed in three stages. He starts by saying in general terms that he prevented humans from 'being smashed apart and going to Hades' (235-6) and that this was the cause of his punishment. He emphasises that his actions were motivated by sympathy and pity (238-41). The chorus commiserate, but (perhaps somewhat confused) ask tentatively why this should have caused such dramatic punishment, which reveals the two further details (*Prometheus Bound* 247-52):

Cho.   You didn't perhaps go even further than this?
Prom. Yes, I stopped mortals foreseeing their death.
Cho.   By finding what cure for this disease?
Prom. I established blind hopes in them.
Cho.   This is a great gift that you gave mortals.
Prom. But what is more, I supplied them with fire.

It is not immediately clear from Prometheus' words whether these two gifts – hope and fire – constitute the preservation of the human race or whether they represent a supplement to that preservation, but the problem (for Zeus) seems to be, notwithstanding short-term succour, that they provide humanity with an open-ended opportunity for advancement.

The concept of hope, however, is the most significant shift from the Hesiodic account. In Hesiod, hope is a distinctly outnumbered counter to the countless ills that have escaped the jar to beset mankind – physical (sickness and disease), moral and spiritual. Here, however, that battery of opposing forces is absent: there is the material world and there is humanity, armed with hope. The explanation that hope is blind, and in particular prevents mortals foreseeing their own death, clearly suggests that hope is what encourages humanity to improve its lot. That is, labour and technology by themselves are not enough. *Prometheus Bound* is not envisaging a 'steady state' of no development, still less that mankind should be so distressed by their own mortality or by only incremental change that they give up.[8]

Prometheus' solution to Zeus' plan is, then, both psychological and material. In Aeschylus fire becomes more than a synonym for livelihood; rather it becomes a powerful metonymy for the idea of progress itself. Fire is said to be a 'teacher of every craft (*tekhnê*) for mortals ... and a great resource' (110-11). Such practical and (implicitly) intellectual advancement needs to be assisted by hope. Without the hope that things can (only) get better, there would be no impulse for change. The capacity for limitless advancement and for control of their own destiny appears to constitute the privileges (*gera*, 107, 229) and honours (*timas*, 30) that Prometheus has passed from gods to men.

Technology and progress

The material dimension is addressed in more detail in the great pair of speeches made by Prometheus to the chorus in the second episode of the play (436-71, 476-506). In the first of these, the rewriting of the Hesiodic account into one of unashamed material and intellectual progress is unequivocal.

Here the comparison of humanity with the gods becomes much clearer. Indeed, Prometheus also claims that he is responsible for the division of privileges for the gods as well (439-40), in the same terms that he has discussed allotting privileges to humanity. The link between the practical and intellectual is central (442-4):

> Listen to the suffering among mortals –
> how they were stupid in earlier days
> and I made them intelligent and achieve sense.

He elaborates: he allowed them to draw inferences (*gnômês*, 456) or speculate on the basis of sense-perception, sight and sound. Without this ability, they wandered around aimlessly (448-9). Earlier men lived like shadows (*oneiratôn*), a striking reversal of the usual Greek notion of mortal ephemerality, which usually sets mortals against the divine and immortal.[9] Here the intellectually-competent humans are the point of contrast. Early man was not more fortunate: rather they lived in caves, like ants, underground.

As well as lifting humanity from the slime, by teaching them building (brick-making and carpentry, 450-1), Prometheus elaborates his gifts in further adaptation and re-interpretation of Hesiod's *Works and Days*, he claims responsibility for understanding weather-signs and times for farming and astronomy (454-8), and the techniques of sailing (467-8). He extends further to the foundational arts of mathematics and writing, the latter, he argues, important for social memory and for music. He claims responsibility for ox-power and horse-power (462-6), and incidentally brings down the horse as 'display of conspicuous consumption by the super-rich' (*agalma tês hyperploutou khlidês*, 466) to the same basic level of animal husbandry, a shift from more elite-aligned poetry.[10]

Prometheus reflects ruefully that despite all these devices, he has no device for escaping his situation. The chorus' sympathetic response compares him to a doctor unable to cure himself, a comment which sets up the second speech, devoted mainly to two specific crafts or skills (*tekhnai*): medicine (478-83) and divination (*mantikê*, 484-99). This pair continue the idea of judgement or discrimination which was seen already in knowing the seasons and the stars. In the case of medicine, the knowledge and judgement on display is explicitly pharmacological, rather than diagnostic. The motif of judgement and discrimination is even more clear in the case of divination: *kakrina* ('and I interpreted', 485); *dyskritous* ('difficult to interpret', 486); *diôris'* ('I distinguished', 489); *dystekmarton* ('difficult to judge', 497). Prometheus runs through most of the different flavours of the technique – dreams, voices, birds, chance meetings, entrails, sacrifices.

Divination might be thought an odd choice, given the stance that Prometheus adopts towards the other gods, but there are a number of factors in play. First, divination was seen as just as much a learned and technical skill (*tekhnê*) as medicine or ship-building, and diviners (*manteis*) were an important part of public life in Athens (even if Aristophanes and other comic writers were to represent them in scathing terms).[11] Interpretation of these signs so as to find out about the state of the world, or about positive and negative implications, was seen on the same level as interpretation of the weather or the stars. To a large extent, these are equivalent to interpreting *nature*. Secondly, in the one place where Prometheus does talk about divine favour or disfavour, he is distinctly reticent about which gods these are, or their status: he uses the rather vaguer term *daimôn* (*daimosin*, 494), which can encompass anything from vague spirits all the way up to Zeus himself. Thirdly, although mortals have been victims of the gods, they are not represented in *Prometheus Bound* as impious (contrast Hesiod). Furthermore, in contrast to writers such as Sophokles or Herodotos, *Prometheus Bound* is considerably more optimistic about the possibility of correct interpretation – and not only with the benefit of hindsight.[12] The prospect of foreknowledge aligns humanity closely with Prometheus himself.

Finally, Prometheus returns to the strictly material, the discovery and use of metals. Given the obvious rewriting of

Hesiod in these speeches, it is not going too far to see in the catalogue of metals a pointed rejection of the myth of races; indeed, in the re-ordering of elements there is a broad reversal of that Hesiodic symbol of decline (502-3):

> bronze, iron, silver, gold: who
> would say that he had discovered them before me?[13]

Prometheus throughout these speeches draws on the tradition of the 'first inventor' (*prôtos heuretês*[14]), as he claims credit for all of them (506). Strictly speaking, though, it is the intellectual capacity and curiosity that he provides, symbolised by fire, that is the source of human development. His claim to have discovered 'skills and means' (477) recalls his earlier description of fire as a teacher (100-1), noted above. The ability of humans to learn, make judgements and draw conclusions is one arm of progress. Having the motivation to lift themselves from the mud is the other.

The materialist turn

Both Prometheus' account of human progress and the removal of the gods as a prime organising narrative draws on the materialist turn in Greek thought, which accelerated from the mid-sixth century onwards, particularly in speculation about the physical nature of the world and its organising principles. This tradition is usually labelled, somewhat inaccurately, as 'presocratic' philosophy. The underlying principle is that human enquiry, by judicious use of evidence and rational argument, can understand the world and its observed phenomena. Attribution of physical causes and effect here leads to an increasingly small role for the gods in what is a broadly material and mechanical approach. As explanations of surface phenomena in terms of physical processes become more complex, there is also a corresponding scepticism about human sense-perceptions.

Such physical accounts of the world develop from the relatively straightforward (if extremely fragmentary) accounts of the Milesians – Thales, Anaximenes and Anaximander – in the sixth century, through to increasingly complex systems with multiple elements proposed in the fifth century by Empedokles, Anaxagoras and the atomists, Demokritos and Leukippos. For the first two (as for some, at least, of the Milesians), there are organising principles or forces, exploiting Greek fondness for personification: thus Empedokles' operating forces are Love and Strife (the latter a reinterpretation of Hesiodic strife(s) which are important for both *Theogony* and, especially, *Works and Days*), while for Anaxagoras, pointedly, it is abstract 'mind' (*Nous*). Demokritos and Leukippos propose the world's first fully-fledged atomic theory without even these vestigial guiding principles. Most, perhaps all, of the pre-atomic theories will have been circulating at the time that *Prometheus Bound* was produced.

In some ways, however, it is the late sixth-century poet Xenophanes (*c.* 570-*c.* 470) who makes clearest the implications of this materialist and rationalist trend in Greek thought, if only for the relatively extensive remains of his poetry, when compared to the Milesians.[15] Xenophanes, himself originally an Ionian, from Kolophon, is clearly aware of Milesian speculation.[16] He himself discusses an array of phenomena in purely material terms (fr. 30):

> The sea is the source of water, and source of wind:
> for there would be no wind without the great sea
> nor streams of rivers nor the rain-water of heaven;
> but the great sea is the producer of clouds and winds
> and rivers.

Whether he had a systematic cosmology is open to doubt, although such matters are also considered in his poetry (fr. 28). He seems to have an evolutionary view of the world and claims that living creatures emerged from or are constituted by mud (frr. 27, 29, 33). One report has him explicitly deriving such views from the observation of fossils (test. 33).

Xenophanes is perhaps more well-known for the assault he

makes on conventional Greek notions of the divine, which seems to be the corollary of these physical observations and speculations. He is the first person we have explicitly to deny that gods take the form of anthropomorphised deities, a belief which he traces back to Homer and Hesiod (frr. 10-13). For Xenophanes the divine is a single entity (frr. 23-4, cf. fr. 26), does not have human form (frr. 14, 23) and acts impersonally through thought (fr. 25). Goddesses such as Iris are merely natural phenomena (the rainbow, fr. 32).[17]

One argument that he repeatedly returns to is that neither the Homeric nor the Hesiodic gods are just in their dealings with each other (let alone humanity) (fr. 11):

> Homer and Hesiod ascribed everything to the gods
> all the things that are the source of curses and abuse
>   among men,
> theft and adultery and deceiving one another.

He is also the first to make the argument against traditional gods on the grounds of their cultural specificity, an observation more well-known from Herodotos' explorations in cultural relativism (3.38). Xenophanes notes that Egyptians and Thracians imagine gods in their own images (fr. 16), and pursues a *reductio ad absurdum* to argue that horses and oxen would have horse-gods and ox-gods respectively (fr. 15).

In intellectual terms, he emphasises the importance of human intellectual effort and enquiry, in spite of the gods, and not because of them (fr. 18):

> Gods did not indeed reveal everything to mortals.
> But as they search it out, in time they find what is
>   better.

Here we see the first articulation of a clearly progressive view in Greek thought and it seems consistent with a heterodox and sceptical view of the divine and of the justice of the conventional Greek gods. A progressive view of human material development is not found explicitly, but would be consistent with his other physical and developmental theories.[18]

Xenophanes and the tradition of enquiry in which he stands were both clearly in play by the time of *Prometheus Bound*, which certainly has a fuller account of enquiry-based progress than that preserved in Xenophanes' fragments. *Prometheus Bound* has a similarly jaundiced view of the inherited gods, but does not *explicitly* go as far as Xenophanes in speculating upon an alternative conception of the divine. Still less does *Prometheus Bound* engage in the scepticism that can be seen in places in Xenophanes. Nor does it adopt the more extreme speculations of Parmenides and his followers who went so far as to deny any change at all. Rather, *Prometheus Bound* is emphatically with those who, in answer to Parmenides, do see change and development. The most relevant of these are Anaxagoras and Empedokles, both active in the mid-fifth century. Anaxagoras certainly had Athenian connections and was associated with Perikles, amongst others. Empedokles' account of change is particularly interesting. His theory of a cosmic cycle of integration and disintegration involved the development of humans through the aggregation of elements, passing through a stage of monstrosity. Precise echoes, however, are harder to pin down.[19]

Above all, though, *Prometheus Bound* is with the mainstream Ionian tradition that the world is there to be interpreted and understood for practical purposes, through a combination of evidence and judgement or theory. This is the approach that underlies Herodotos' *History* (Ionian *historiê* = 'enquiry') and the tradition of ethnography and geographical enquiry in which he in part sits. It is also that which underlies contemporary medicine, in mid-fifth-century treatises ascribed to Hippokrates, such as *Airs, Waters, Places*.

The language of medicine permeates *Prometheus Bound* and is not restricted to Prometheus' second speech on progress. It features particularly in the exchanges between Prometheus and Okeanos (377-85). Okeanos refers to the anger of Zeus as a sickness (*nosousas*) and describes words as metaphorical doctors. Prometheus' response uses the technical language of medicine and presocratic thought to cap this rather glib remark (379-90):

> Yes, if one softens a heart at the right time
> and doesn't forcibly (*biai*) dry out a swelling spirit.

A rather different take on the idea of healing words comes in the Io scene, where Io's affliction easily attracts the language of sickness (596, 606), as does the pain of Prometheus' torture (43, 146, 268-9, 274-6) and the destruction of the human race (249, above). Prometheus' revelation of Io's future comes only after the chorus have inspired an investigation of Io's disease (*historêsômen noson*), Io has attacked platitudes as 'the most shameful disease' (685-6) and the chorus have again pressed Prometheus to ease the suffering of the sick (698-9); this scene, then, demonstrates the right time and process for such verbal intervention.

Okeanos' language of investigation, sight and seeing, along with his self-deprecatory reference to his 'illness' of wanting to help Prometheus, all point to Okeanos as using the language of Ionian philosophy, science and medicine, albeit perhaps only at a superficial level. A more aggressive set of exchanges are to be seen in the Hermes episode, where Hermes accuses Prometheus of madness and sickness, rejected by the Titan (977-8) and again (*maniôn*, 1057) rejected angrily by the chorus in their final intervention: it is betrayal, for them, that is the worst sickness (1068-70). Prometheus had earlier referred (225) to the lack of trust as the sickness (*nosêma*) of tyranny.[20]

The language of sickness and disease is only the most obvious debt to ancient medicine. The concept of material, as well as intellectual, progress can also clearly be traced there. One early (probably late fifth-century) medical treatise, [Hippokrates], *On Ancient Medicine* 3 itself theorised human progress in strictly material terms. Here the cause of progress, encompassing technical developments in food and farming, is brought under the over-arching concept of medicine:

I think that in the beginning man too had a similar diet [sc. to animals]. The means that have now been discovered and contrived (*tetekhnêmena*) I think came about later. For they suffered many terrible things because of their violent and beast-like way of life, gathering raw, unmixed and very robust food. Such things they would suffer now too, encountering violent afflictions, diseases and, swiftly, death.[21]

Such a progressive materialist view was clearly well-established by the 420s, appropriated for various re-tellings and even sent up in comedy,[22] but it can be traced back further until at least the 440s.

One of the fullest accounts of human progress, which is generally taken to derive from a fifth-century source is found in Diodorus Siculus' *Universal History* 1.8.1-9.[23] This account has many echoes of the account in *Prometheus Bound*, although it includes a social dimension that is more implicit in Prometheus' speech. In the Diodoran account, humans come together against the depredations of animals and are forced to communicate with each other. This leads to the development of language by a series of *ad hoc* agreements within communities (compare *Prometheus Bound*'s interest in numeracy and literacy). Need drives change, but, as with the Promethean account, humanity has the facility of reasoning and sense in order to respond to that pressure (*Universal History* 1.8.5-8[24]):

(They say that) thus the first humans led lives full of trouble, as none of the useful devices for livelihood had been discovered, they lacked clothing, had no experience of construction and of fire, and were wholly ignorant of benign food. Accordingly, as they were ignorant of the effects of a wild diet, they made no allowances for the need for crops; and so many of them died in winter because of the cold and the inadequacy of their diet. As a result of this, they gradually learnt by experience to take refuge in caves during winter and to store up whatever crops could be preserved. Little by little they learnt about fire and the rest of what was useful, crafts (*tekhnas*) too were learnt and everything else that was able to contribute to the livelihood of all.

The identity of the source of these ideas is disputed. One theory is that this goes back to Demokritos of Abdera (born 460-57), whose thought encompassed many fields beyond physics and metaphysics. For Demokritos, 'necessity' caused the arts (fr. 144).[25] Whether that is right or not (and Demokritos is probably too late to influence *Prometheus Bound* on any dating), it seems clear that looking for a 'first inventor' of the notion of progress is mistaken: such views are clearly developing out of related traditions of enquiry in the period.

The social turn

There is, however, one thinker who is of particular importance for *Prometheus Bound*: Protagoras of Abdera (*c.* 490-*c.* 420 BCE), probably an older contemporary of his fellow Abderite Demokritos.[26] Protagoras, according to tradition, was the first of the 'sophists', thinkers and teachers who moved from city to city charging for their teaching. Protagoras had provocative and shocking things to say in a variety of fields – epistemology (theory of knowledge), rhetoric and ethics – using strongly relativist and sceptical principles. Protagoras it was who argued that there were two sides to every question – the 'weaker' and 'stronger' arguments, as mocked by Aristophanes in *Clouds*. He argued that 'man was the measure of all things' (fr. 1), which in its original context referred to perception and reality (subjective perceptions are true for the perceiver). As far as the gods are concerned, he professed agnosticism (fr. 4). His overall pitch, though, was that he delivered *political* education. This is the topic of Plato's dialogue, *Protagoras*, where the sophist is presented as defending the idea that political excellence can be taught. His first argument in favour of this uses an allegorical myth – a myth of Prometheus and human progress (320d-322d).[27]

In this version Prometheus and his not-at-all-clever brother Epimetheus are responsible for assigning qualities to different species, primarily resources for survival (offensive and defensive resources, 320d-321b). Unfortunately Epimetheus forgot to give any such resources to the human race, who were left 'naked, unshod, uncovered and unarmed' (321c). This was the reason why Prometheus stole fire from Hephaistos and Athena, in order to provide humans with expertise in crafts (*entekhnon sophian*, 321d) and thus plentiful resources for living (*euporeian ... tou biou*, 322a). With this facility, they invent a set of skills, most of which are familiar from *Prometheus Bound* and other progressive accounts – language, building, clothing, footwear, blankets and crops (322a). They also invent gods, altars and sacrifice (compare divination in *Prometheus Bound*).[28]

There is, however, a catch: humans have the skills to develop a material living (skill in handicrafts, *dêmiourgikê tekhnê*), but they lack political skill (*politikê tekhnê*). They try to come together in defence against wild animals (warfare here seen as a political skill), but are unable to establish any social cohesion. They mistreat one another, the proto-cities break up and they once again become vulnerable. Political skill, according to Protagoras, belongs with Zeus (321d), and so in this version it is Zeus that fears for mankind and sends Hermes to give them *aidôs* (shame or respect[29]) and justice (*dikê*).

The point to the *mythos* is this. Hermes asks Zeus whether political skills should be distributed like handicraft skills, with different people being expert in different skills. Zeus' reply is that social and political skills should be given to all (Plato, *Protagoras* 322d) :

'To all,' said Zeus, ' and let all have a share in them: for cities would not exist, if few men had a share in them as in other skills; and make this a rule from me that whoever is not able to have a share in respect (*aidôs*) and justice (*dikê*) should be killed, as they are a disease for the city.'

Protagoras elaborates the political message: advice on technical or craft-related matters is sought from experts, but political advice, which consists of justice, can come from anyone. The implications for his own trade are that if everyone has a basic political and social skill or capacity, which he sums up as justice (*dikaiosynê*) and good sense (*sôphrosynê*, 323a), then he as a professional teacher can develop that skill. Almost incidentally, this also constitutes an argument for general public participation in politics, an argument for democracy. If the arguments that Plato puts into the mouth of his Protagoras reflect those of the actual Protagoras, this would seem to have been the earliest developed argument for democracy of which we know.[30]

The combination of Prometheus with an account of material progress has led many scholars to connect this account with *Prometheus Bound*. There are also smaller points of contact – Prometheus' motivation in Plato is to stop humanity from being annihilated (*aistôtheiê* 321a, cf. *Prometheus Bound* 151, 232, 668); there is a shared emphasis on this being a divine privilege to which humans are given access (as above); and it is a privilege particularly associated with Hephaistos (321d, cf. *Prometheus Bound* 36-8). Indeed, the ending of the trilogy has even been connected with the dedication of the Temple of Hephaistos and Athena above the agora in the 440s.[31] A narrative arc similar to that which is offered in Plato also might help to resolve some of the issues in the developing trilogy. Thus, an explanation for why Prometheus and Zeus come to terms in *Prometheus Unbound* may be because the human race are suffering through a lack of political skill and thus Zeus has an additional bargaining chip to set against Prometheus' knowledge of his potential future. The role of Hermes at the end of *Prometheus Bound*, as an agent of *Realpolitik*, would make him suitable for reprising that role in bringing *dikê* to humans in *Prometheus Unbound* or a third play. If Zeus were to initiate (or offer) this, then an Aeschylean association of Zeus with *dikê* might be engineered at the end of the trilogy; what is more, the progressive and teleological nature of human political development would look very similar to the legal progress achieved in the *Eumenides*. If, as I argued in the previous chapter, the vehemently anti-tyrannical language of *Prometheus Bound* has particular resonance within the democratic ideology at Athens, a final aetiology for democratic participation would fit thematically – the positive argument for democracy following the assault on its opposite.

There are, however, many points of disagreement between the Promethean stories of *Prometheus Bound* and *Protagoras*. Epimetheus plays no part whatsoever in *Prometheus Bound*. There is some evidence in *Prometheus Bound* of Prometheus assigning privileges to gods, but no evidence of he or his brother doing the same for living creatures. Prometheus' theft in *Prometheus Bound* is a response to Zeus threatening to wipe out the human race, not the result of his brother's foolishness. Prometheus is characterised in *Protagoras* more like the Hesiodic trickster than the heroic Aeschylean figure – Prometheus sneaks the fire away from Hephaistos and Athena because he is scared of Zeus' guards. The punishment highlighted by Plato's Protagoras is not chaining to either pillar or rock, but the punishment via Epimetheus, i.e. the gift of Pandora. In these respects, the Protagorean myth is a far *less* revisionist account than that of *Prometheus Bound*. There is also absolutely no sign in *Prometheus Bound*, as yet, that Zeus has any kind of privileged guardianship of political skills – unless, that is, they involve violence. So if there is a connection between the two Promethean accounts of progress, it is not a direct one. Of course, given the very few remaining fragments of Protagoras' own writing, we do not know how much creative rewriting has been undertaken by Plato. Either the distinction between political and non-political skills (compare the Diodoran passage where social skills are included within technical progress) or the manner of that distinction may have been introduced by Plato.

A further argument against any straightforward adoption of the story-arc of *Protagoras* is that *Prometheus Bound* suggests that the humans are not restricted from living social lives or, indeed, political ones. As with the Diodoran account and in contrast to that of Plato's Protagoras, the skills learnt in

Prometheus Bound do have a social dimension – not least writing and music – and also imply settled communities: farming (in a much more organised form) and sailing. In addition, it seems clear that humans are living in ordered communities by the time of Io's arrival – her expulsion by Inakhos is from such a community – and they will live for thirteen more generations without coming to the verge of destruction in the apocalyptic fashion of *Protagoras*. Any introduction of *dikê* and *sôphrosynê* into the *Prometheus Bound* story arc would have to be more limited. The removal of internal strife (*stasis*) might be a strong possibility, in particular a move to include all the citizens within the political process. This would give a suitably Athenian and democratic flavour to the conclusion, while matching the ideological thrust of the Protagorean story.

Protagorean influences in Greek tragedy of the middle of the fifth century are entirely plausible. Protagoras was at the height of his powers in the 440s, and was asked to write the laws for the foundation of the city of Thourioi, an Athenian colony but with strong panhellenic associations (probably 443 BCE). A non-Promethean but undeniably Protagorean account of human progress is put into the mouth of the chorus of Sophokles' *Antigone*, of c. 442. Here, in the first stasimon (334-75) the 'man is the measure of all things' doctrine of Protagoras is interpreted in terms of human progress. 'There are many amazing things, and none more amazing than man …' (334). Sailing, ploughing, hunting, talking, thinking, government and medicine are all mentioned, a similar range of material and social elements.[32] It is not impossible to conceive of Protagoras' philosophical activity beginning in the 460s, which would even allow for him to be influencing late Aeschylus.

By the time of *Antigone*, however, it is already possible to see the backlash against Protagorean ideas. The larger question posed by Protagoras' provocation is not only whether material development implies social and political development, but whether that social development has any fixed foundations, is actually beneficial, or offers any insight into how humans *ought* to behave. If there is no place for the gods in human development, what kind of anchor can there be for Greek ethics? The chorus in *Antigone* provide a number of cautions to a purely materialist approach – man has not conquered death, and he needs to honour both the chthonic laws and the gods (*Antigone* 365-76):

> With some cleverness, the device of craft (*to mêkhanoen*
>   *tekhnas*) beyond expectation,
> he sometimes goes to the bad, at other times to the good.
> If he respects the laws of the earth
> and the justice of the gods held in binding oaths,
> his city prospers: he is an outcast (*apolis*), whoever
>   provides a home
> for wickedness to satisfy his recklessness (*tolmas*).
> May he never be at my hearth
> nor have equal status, whoever does these things.

The chorus are suggesting that there are fixed points for human behaviour and limits to materialism.

This debate, the so-called *nomos-physis* debate – law or convention (*nomos*) against nature (*physis*) – becomes the battleground for Greek ethical and political theory in the latter part of the fifth century. The chorus represent one broadly conservative reaction. Within 'sophistic' circles, acceptance of the conventional nature of human behaviour and law had dramatically different political implications. On the Protagorean wing, law is broadly utilitarian and democratic. Societies come together to provide protection, either against animals or other groups of humans or powerful individuals. Other interpretations held that because human law was arbitrary and that human society was naturally (*physei*) dominated by the most powerful, the most powerful ought to be in charge. This has obvious attractions for an oligarchic (or monarchical) position, but it could also be used to justify powerful individual politicians within a democratic context (so Kallikles in Plato's *Gorgias*) and the actions of democracies within international politics (so the Athenians in the so-called 'Melian Dialogue' of

3. Technology and Civilisation

Thucydides 5.85-111). Still others denied any value to acting ethically at all, given that ethical norms were arbitrary and conventional (so Thrasymakhos in the first book of Plato's *Republic*); again this could be used to justify revolutionary and anti-democratic behaviour.

It is not obvious that *Prometheus Bound* is making an intervention into the height of that conflict, so much as firing an opening salvo. There are undoubtedly, however, strong hints of the burgeoning sophistic movement. One is the emphasis on speech, as seen above in Okeanos' contribution. Some of the abstract vocabulary of *Prometheus Bound* is also suggestive of the emerging discourse, such as craft (*tekhnê*), device (*mêkhanêma*, 469, and cognates) and invention (*sophisma*, 459, 470), the distinction between speech and reality (*logôi/ergôi*, 336, 1080). Other language is more broadly consonant with the inquiry-led approaches to the world that I discussed earlier.[33]

Most striking of all is the introduction of the term *sophistês* in some of its earliest appearances in surviving Greek literature at both the beginning and end of the play. Kratos explains to Hephaistos that the point of the punishment is for Prometheus to 'learn that, though a *sophistês*, he is slower than Zeus'. Likewise, Hermes opens his indictment of Prometheus with the address, 'Hey, you *sophistês*, ...' (944). The first instance is sarcastic, but suggests that Zeus is a greater *sophistês*, the latter unambiguously negative. The term does not seem to be used in the technical sense of a professional teacher; rather it seems to be used in a similar sense to that in Kratinos' comedy, *Arkhilokhos and Friends*, which seems to have had a chorus of thinkers, made up wholly or mostly of poets (or their adherents). One character observes of this chorus, 'What a swarm of *sophistai* you stirred up' (fr. 2). Such people are dealers in wisdom (*sophia*) and are engaged in public discourse, but in no sense limited to philosophers or teachers in a narrow sense.[34] *Prometheus Bound*'s account of human progress is entirely compatible with that emergent sense of social and political enquiry.

Philosophy and tragedy

Prometheus Bound offers intellectual provocation on a number of different levels. The characters, as I have discussed, present a series of models with which the audience are invited to compare themselves, to identify with or to reject, all of which have political implications. Prometheus himself, as well as offering a personal model, also provides the means for mankind's intellectual, social and technical progress. The emphasis on humanity's own endeavours combined with the assault on the justice of the Olympian gods does not, in the first instance, encourage an atheist position so much as a profoundly materialist one, but it does open up further kinds of theological scepticism.

Even without considering the possible outcomes of the trilogy, it is tempting to draw together the two strands: the highly politicised freedom of speech and thought which Prometheus defiantly maintains (against Okeanos in particular) with the material and social progress outlined in his great speeches. The productive elision in those speeches, between fire as enabler of human skills on the one hand and Prometheus as provider of those skills on the other, suggests that Promethean qualities are intrinsic to human progress. The implication is that access to knowledge and freedom to learn and the harnessing of hope for social improvement are the corollary of political freedom in general and democratic freedom in particular.

That Prometheus and progress are explicitly tied to an inclusive political agenda in Plato's *Protagoras* supports the view that in the Prometheus trilogy the explanations of material and political progress are intertwined. As I have argued, however, the relationship between *Prometheus Bound* and *Protagoras* is not straightforward. *Prometheus Bound* maintains a social focus and, indeed, is suspicious of powerful individuals, whereas *Protagoras* explains the education of a wealthy elite to be political players. *Prometheus Bound* maintains the aggressive language of radical democracy where *Protagoras* is much more abstracted and distanced. *Prometheus Bound* is certainly engaging fully with contemporary Greek thought, but it is far more than the dramatisation of a Protagorean line of argument. Rather, *Prometheus Bound* is making its own political and social intervention, on dramatic, narrative and symbolic levels, in far stronger and more specific terms. Indeed, while *Prometheus Bound* is clearly engaging with contemporary accounts of intellectual, material and social progress, the radical democratic account of progress is its own specific contribution to that ongoing debate.

4

Making a Spectacle

Prometheus Bound is perhaps the most visually arresting of Greek tragedies. This has not always won it friends, indeed has often been held to detract from the essence of tragedy. The visual effects are undeniably spectacular, but comparable at root to those of Aeschylean and post-Aeschylean drama and well-integrated into the thematic concerns of the play. There are some well-worn problems of staging, but difficulties have been exaggerated. In this chapter, I discuss the dramaturgical techniques which set a central stationary pivot against a variety of surrounding movement, the use of sung and spoken narrative to extend chronological and geographical scope, and the self-conscious demands placed on the audience in responding to the spectacle.

Objections to *Prometheus Bound*'s use of stage effects derive from Aristotle's *Poetics*, which ranked the elements of Greek tragedy in importance. Plot was his highest concern, followed by character and ideas. Bringing up the rear were more performative elements: language, song and the visual dimension (*opsis*). Spectacle and song are, Aristotle argues, to do with pleasure (*Poetics* 1450b):

> Spectacle (*opsis*) can beguile the mind (*psykhagôgikon*) but is not intrinsic to poetry. The art of the prop-maker is much more effective in creating visual effects than the art of poets.

Aristotle goes on to concede that pity and fear can be caused by spectacle, but argues that they are better deriving from plot:

terrifying (*to phoberon*) and monstrous elements (*to teratôdes*) (1453b) do not contribute to tragedy. He warns about the difficulty of representing amazing (*thaumaston*), improbable (*alogon*) events visually and the danger of provoking humour (1460a). At 1455b-1456a, he discusses four types of tragedy – complex (based on recognition and reversal), emotional (*pathêtikê*), character-based (*êthikê*) and a fourth type, which may (although the crucial word is corrupt) be spectacle-based.[1] As examples, he singles out *Prometheus*, the *Daughters of Phorkys* (the Graiai) and 'plays set in Hades'. These all involve gods, monsters or a non-earthly environment, which seem to fit the characteristics of drama driven by spectacle. All are consistent with Aeschylean output.[2] Theatrical innovation and strong visual effects are central to the understanding of Aeschylus in antiquity, even in Aristophanes' *Frogs*. Later tradition included colourfully implausible anecdotes, such as the *Eumenides* causing vomiting and miscarriages. Spectacle is associated with such non-human entities.[3]

Although critics have been increasingly interested in performance,[4] they have been increasingly reluctant to associate Aeschylus with spectacle. Oliver Taplin, in particular, pared down Aeschylean staging as much as possible and removed the crowds of extras and other effects foisted on Aeschylus by earlier critics who saw spectacle as central to his oeuvre without always much sense of the consequences for performance. Taplin's conviction that *Prometheus Bound* is not by Aeschylus is rooted in this project. The play is certainly grandstanding, but there are also more subtle effects at work, and both emotional and cognitive interest. Neither are alien to the technique of the dramatist who conjured up the *Agamemnon* tapestry walk (905-74) or the threatened mass suicide of the *Suppliant Women* (455-67).

Conditions of production

Plays in Athens were produced in the Theatre of Dionysos, nestling in the south-east slopes of the Acropolis. The visible remains of the theatre are primarily Hellenistic and Roman remodelling of the fourth-century stone theatre of Lykourgos; the fifth-century theatre was less grand. By the late fifth century, the only stone elements were the front row of seats for dignitaries (*proedria*) and, possibly, stone foundations for a stage building (*skênê*, literally 'shed'). Seating for the bulk of the theatre was made of temporary wooden stands (*ikria*) set into the hillside. A fully stone version may not have been built until its remodelling by Lykourgos in the later fourth century. Latest research suggests that an upper area of seating was only added in the fourth century, and thus formal capacity was around 6-7,000 people, far less than the later Lykourgan or Hellenistic theatres.[5]

The main performance space was the dancing-floor (*orkhêstra*) of compacted earth, which was a roughly rectangular or trapezoidal space. This shape is known from other Attic theatres of the period, notably that at Thorikos.[6] In earlier drama, the *orkhêstra* functioned as a general performance space, not only for dancing. Entrance and exit were by two side entrances (*eisodoi* [singular *eisodos*] as they were known at the time; later as *parodoi* [*parodos*]). By 458, the stage building (*skênê*) had been added, which often represented a palace or other building and served as an additional point of ingress and egress, provided a visual focus and probably also assisted with sound projection. The *skênê* also provided a flat roof, most often used for divine entries. No play of Aeschylus before the *Oresteia* requires the stage building. Scenery, decoration of the *skênê* (*skênographia*) was reputedly introduced by Sophokles and may have been available for late Aeschylus. A low stage may have been in use by the 420s and may have been introduced with the *skênê* itself, but there is no conclusive evidence for this. Over the course of the fifth century, there was an increasing demarcation in tragedy between actors and chorus (stage and *orkhêstra*), but this is unlikely to have affected *Prometheus Bound*.

Plays were all performed in masks, with actors playing multiple roles. Typical tragic dress for male characters consisted of long, ornate (or patterned) robes, rather than the shorter, plainer tunic (*khitôn*), which was ordinary wear. During Aeschylus' career, the number of actors had risen from one (interacting with the chorus) to three. Aeschylus is credited with the expansion from one to two actors; the third variously ascribed to Sophokles or Aeschylus. Certainly, early fifth-century theatre was in rapid development. Some Aeschylean plays – especially *Persians*, *Seven* and *Suppliant Women* – demonstrate the technique of single actor engaging with chorus and chorus-leader; this technique is also used in *Prometheus Bound*, particularly in the parodos and first episode. It is rare even in late Aeschylus to have three actors on stage at the same time, but it does happen in every play of the *Oresteia*. Three-cornered discussions were still largely avoided, which may show that their use was still early in development.[7] Three actors are only required in the opening scene of *Prometheus Bound*.

There were two special effects available to the fifth-century Athenian theatre, both of which required the creation of the *skênê*. Firstly, the *ekkyklêma* ('the thing that is rolled out'), a wheeled platform that could be pushed out from the central door of the *skênê* served primarily as a means of displaying interior scenes to the audience. Its earliest use is likely to be in *Agamemnon* where Klytaimestra displays the dead bodies of Agamemnon and Kassandra to the audience (1372-99).[8] Secondly, the crane (*mêkhanê*, literally 'device') displayed flying characters, either riding a flying creature – as Bellerophon and Pegasos (in Euripides' *Bellerophon*), parodied as Trygaios on giant dung beetle in Aristophanes' *Peace* (422/1) – or self-powered, like Perseus and his winged sandals (Euripides' *Andromeda*, sent up in Aristophanes' *Women at the Thesmophoria*, 412/1). The crane seems to have been a relatively simple piece of kit: a long arm with a counterweight, which lifted actors over the *skênê* and into the performance area; mounting and dismounting took place out of sight behind the stage-building. Its earliest datable use was in *Medea* (431).[9] The *mêkhanê* certainly and, I will argue, the *ekkyklêma* are required for the staging of *Prometheus Bound*. It has sometimes been suggested that the theatre at

Syracuse had a greater range of effects, which could have been used for *Prometheus Bound*, but evidence is lacking and the Sicilian hypothesis not compelling.[10]

Finally, Athenian theatre under the democracy appears to have been a much more broadly based form of mass entertainment than theatre today. Attendances of 6-7,000 would represent a fifth to a quarter of the citizen population, even allowing for attendance by children, metics (resident foreigners), non-residents and foreign ambassadors and (probably) women. Attendance was comparable with the citizen assembly, numerically and ideologically.[11] There was a charge for the theatre – two obols – and although Perikles is said by Plutarch to have introduced the 'theoric fund' which subsidised tickets for the poor, there is no good evidence for its existence before the fourth century and it is extremely unlikely to have applied during Aeschylus' lifetime. How far ticket prices affected demand for the theatre and skewed attendance is unclear, but even an audience composed heavily of zeugites or better-off thetes would put the mass audience, both materially and conceptually, at a considerable distance from the elite families that dominate Greek tragedy.[12]

Focus and movement

The principal visual effect is the crucifixion of Prometheus. I will consider first what actually happens on stage and then the impact on the audience. Prometheus is evidently brought on through one of the *eisodoi*, with Kratos and Bia as close guards and Hephaistos in attendance. Prometheus is set upright (32) against a high, rocky cliff (4-5) or hill (*pagos*, 20) which presents a cleft or chasm (*pharangi*, 15). Hephaistos fastens iron or steel bands over his arms (55-63) and legs (76-81), bored through (76) so that they can be attached to the rocks with metal pegs. These are relatively straightforwardly staged, but the most shocking punishment is more problematic. There is, however, no mistaking what Kratos is telling Hephaistos to do (64-5):

Now, nail the obdurate, biting point of a steel spike
right through his chest with all your strength.

In addition to the spike, there are bands around Prometheus'
chest, similarly bored through and nailed to the rock (71). The
punishment echoes the Athenian punishment of *apotympanis-
mos*, whereby criminals were strapped to a board, with throat
rather than chest bands. Indeed, any theatrical realisation
would probably have involved strapping to a wooden board.[13]

Where in the performance space is this done and how? A
central position is most theatrically plausible. The dominant
area of the space is the centre of the *orkhêstra*, but there are
problems with placing Prometheus there: he has to be attached
to something. Traditionally, Prometheus is attached to a *pillar*
(Hesiod, *Theogony* 521), which would be manageable as portable scenery, but a cliff is another matter. It may not be
impossible: one of the earliest depictions of Greek drama, the
so-called Basel dancers, seems to represent a tragic chorus
attending a character rising out of a tomb (Fig. 4.1),[14] but
Prometheus' rock is an order of magnitude further. Nor would
it easily suggest a cleft or chasm. Something that substantial
would also restrict views of the performance space.[15] A better
solution is that Prometheus was attached to the *skênê* building
in the central doorway, which could suggest a chasm or cleft, as
well as providing something for Prometheus to be nailed
against. The stage-building provides a plausible cliff. It certainly does not need to be represented literally: the theory
proposed by Hammond, that a rocky outcrop at the eastern edge
of the *orkhêstra* still existed and was used for rocky landscapes
in Aeschylean tragedy is over-literal and is dramatically im-
practical.[16]

The staging of the spike would require a moderate degree of
theatrical sleight-of-hand to create a plausible (and loud metal-
on-metal) transfixion. If, as with the leg and arm bands, the
spike is notionally fixed through the band, there is scope for
such legerdemain. There is absolutely no need to resort to a
theory popular with German scholarship of the nineteenth and

Fig. 4.1. 'Basel dancers': Attic red-figure column krater, *c.* 480. Antikenmuseum Basel und Sammlung Ludwig, inv. BS415. Photo: Andreas F. Voegelin.

early twentieth centuries that Prometheus was played by a larger-than-human size dummy (voiced from behind the *skênê* or from an actor hidden inside).[17]

A central doorway position may be suggested by a South Italian vase painting clearly influenced by *Prometheus Unbound* (Fig. 4.2), in which Prometheus is attached to an arch-like rock. Herakles appears (to his left), as perhaps do other characters from the play.[18]

The underlying dramatic idea is tension between the pinioned Prometheus and the various visitors who will interact with him: Hephaistos and Kratos; the chorus; Okeanos; Io; Hermes. The closest analogy for this kind of effect in Greek tragedy is Sophokles' *Ajax* (*c.* 450), where Ajax's body provides a strong visual focus following his suicide. Like Prometheus, Ajax is run through on stage, this time by Hektor's sword. Ajax is the reminder of a fallen hero; Prometheus, isolated and suffering, displays the effects of

Fig. 4.2. Prometheus Unbound: Apulian red-figure calyx krater, c. 340. Berlin: Antikensammlung, 1969.9. © bpk/Antikensammlung, SMB/Johannes Laurentius.

tyrannical power – reinforced through thematic use of the language of yoking and binding[19] – but also symbolises his resistance. The interaction of other characters with his suffering body sustains theatrical interest and variety and explores visually their different kinds of relationships. This kind of stark visual symbol can be seen throughout Aeschylus' dramaturgy, from Darius' ghost in *Persians* through the suppliants' threat to hang themselves from the images of the gods in *Suppliant Women* to the tapestries in *Agamemnon* and the chorus of Erinyes in *Eumenides*, all of which, like the pinioned Prometheus, are doing a great deal of dramatic work.[20]

Spectacle and engagement

The most spectacular effects follow in the arrival of the chorus in the parodos and Okeanos in the second half of the first episode. Prometheus, left by Kratos, Bia and Hephaistos steadies himself after switching between speech and song. Then he breaks into an exclamation (114-17) :

Ah! Ah! Eagh! Eagh!
What was that noise? What was that smell that rushed
    up to me unseen?
Was it sent by a god, human, or something in-between,
to reach this rock at the end of the earth?

Prometheus calls on the unknown visitor or visitors to witness his sufferings, but clearly cannot see them. In alarm and distress, he hears a movement of wings, thinking that they are birds (124-6), which may hint at the well-known eagle.[21] He shudders at what approaches (*to proserpon*, 127). The chorus then enter.

Prometheus' apparent unsightedness at 114-27, and the description of the chorus as flying, have led to a variety of stagings, many of which are highly implausible. The chorus describe themselves as a 'formation' (*taxis*, 128-9), with 'competing (or eager) wings' (*pterygôn thoais hamillais*, 129-30), but also describe themselves as coming 'unshod, in a winged vehicle' (*apedilos okhôi apterôi*, 135). They apparently continue in this vehicle or vehicles until 272, when Prometheus invites them to step to the ground, and at 277-81 the chorus describe themselves as having nimbly left their 'swift-winged seat' (*kraipnosyton thakon*, 289) and the realm of the birds and as approaching the rocky land. At this point, Okeanos appears, also flying, on a fantastic flying creature. The chorus do not speak again until the first stasimon (397), when Okeanos has departed, whereupon they seem to resume their interaction with Prometheus.

The staging of the chorus presents two sets of permutations, depending on how literally the text is enacted. First, their vehicle could be:

1. a large single wagon-like vehicle
2. multiple single-seater vehicles
3. entirely imaginary

and they could enter

1. by means of the crane (*mêkhanê*)
2. by appearing on the *skênê* roof, disappearing at 284 and entering the *orkhêstra* on foot for the first stasimon
3. by dancing into the *orkhêstra*

Although ancient commentators put the chorus on the crane, there is no evidence from the fifth century that the crane could support the weight or numbers needed to transport the chorus. Two individuals are the most carried elsewhere.[22] Twelve (for an Aeschylean chorus, probably) or fifteen (as regularly later) seems an implausible up-rating in specification.[23] More than one conveyance per crane, or more than one crane, is a recipe for chaos.[24] Use of the crane seems ruled out.

Use of the roof[25] has been held to explain the lack of interaction between the chorus and Okeanos, and why Prometheus cannot see the chorus when they enter. Dramatic convention and practical mechanics argue against. Elsewhere, a choral exit mid-play (as in *Ajax* and *Eumenides*) entails a change of scene, although it could be argued that the chorus have not yet entered at all. There is also an issue of weight and space, particularly if the chorus dance during their songs, as normal. The *skênê* roof is usually used for much smaller groups. Both space and weight tell against an actual conveyance rather than something more costume-like (or imaginary). A fundamental objection to the choral entrance on the roof is simply this: although Prometheus cannot see the chorus before they start singing, once they arrive he can see them well enough to determine who they are (136-40), he expects them to see him (140-3) and they evidently can

89

do so (144). If Prometheus is attached to the *skênê* or to a large central prop, there is absolutely no way that he could see the chorus; nor they him. The roof cannot hold.

The chorus must enter at ground level. The fact that Prometheus cannot see them, but can hear and smell them, before they start singing is not intrinsically problematic with a central Prometheus, particularly as he is in considerable distress. There is certainly no need to be over-precise: the chorus do not have to appear on the very brink of the *orkhêstra* at the moment that Prometheus has finished speaking at 127. He ends with terror at an approaching noise. To follow this with the approach of the chorus up the *eisodos* (with or without music) works entirely in favour of the staging-effects and not against them.

Finally, the chorus' supposedly flying entry is described overwhelmingly in terms of speed (125-6, 129, 132, 279). Speed suggests that the large omnibus conveyance often proposed is as unlikely in wheeled as in aerial form. Entrance as a group is also suggested by their self-description as a 'formation' (*taxis*, 128-9). As well as speed, the notional carriages supposedly have the occupant(s) barefoot and seated. As Fraenkel has argued, something akin to the single-seater conveyance associated with Triptolemos seems to be imagined.[26] This rickshaw-like model sometimes appears explicitly winged as well as wheeled. Some are pulled, others' locomotive force is unclear: one instance has Dionysos pulled by a satyr.[27] These light buggies, whether pulled by supernumeraries or (less likely) by animals, are the most plausible of the literal carriage options. If so, the buggies would likely be removed after 283, when the chorus have stepped out of them.

Such an entrance would undoubtedly be spectacular and wheeled entrances are not unknown for actors – indeed, the chariot entrance is a feature of Aeschylean spectacle. Whether twelve (or fifteen) such entrances are acceptable is largely a matter of taste, but the idea of a rickshaw ballet has not appealed to everyone.[28] The alternative is that these sort of conveyances are being described but left to the audience's imagination and not presented literally. Choral movement, music and dance would convey the idea of flight. Certainly, this is no stately entrance of marching anapaests as elsewhere in Aeschylus (*Persians*, *Suppliant Women*, *Agamemnon*). The first pair of strophes from the chorus are iambo-choriambic, the second iambic and dactylic: easy, flowing movement but not over-quick. The advantage of the mimetic dance above all is that it can reinforce the rhythm of flying in a way not open even to the most nimble carriage.[29] Visual movement again reinforces and is reinforced by thematic language and imagery.[30]

Objections to a mimetic dance mostly point to the insistence on the details of both carriage and flight, particularly at the moment of entry and in Prometheus' invitation to the chorus to descend, together with their response.[31] In fact, there is a paradox in any reconstruction of fifth-century staging. As a rule of thumb, significant stage action is encoded in the text, but not only are there occasions where this is clearly not the case (as below), but the reverse – that all description is enacted – certainly cannot hold.[32] An explanation of the chorus' rapid arrival is certainly needed. The best parallel for a flying chorus, in Aristophanes' *Clouds*, has a number of features in common with *Prometheus Bound*. The chorus start singing (presumably in the *eisodos* over forty lines before they are seen by the characters, when their horizontal approach is described as descending towards the performance area (323). The other famed winged comic chorus, in *Birds* remains thoroughly grounded throughout.[33] Overall, I am inclined to think that the chorus' flight in *Prometheus Bound* was executed through the medium of dance – and none the less spectacular for that.

The next entrance, by Okeanos, is also a flying entrance, but in this instance its profile fits perfectly with the crane. Okeanos enters astride a flying creature, which he describes as a swift-winged, four-legged bird (286, 395). He is riding it like a horse, albeit without bit or bridle (287). The scholia claim that it is a griffin, and this may be right.[34] This matches comic parodies of tragic flight which explicitly draw attention to the convention of the crane (as above). The conclusion of Euripides' *Medea* was similar, albeit in a flying snake-drawn chariot. Absence of song makes mimetic dance unlikely for Okeanos. A crane entry is well within the spectrum of practicality and theatrical convention, and also resolves some problems identified in this scene, in particular that Okeanos does not talk to his daughters or vice-versa. There is certainly no suggestion in the text that Okeanos dismounts; his dismissal by Prometheus has him leaving without delay (391-6).

In comparable scenes, where the character is dangling in mid-air above the *orkhêstra*, interactions with the chorus are rare, and indeed the conversations between actors are circumscribed. Medea addresses and interacts with Jason (*Medea* 1317-1414); Trygaios interacts with a slave and then his daughter, in sequence; in *Women at the Thesmophoria*, the brief aerial interaction is between Euripides and the archer. It is important not to underestimate the difficulties in managing complex interactions from the air – Trygaios' fears for his safety in *Peace* 173-5 are a joke, but reflect how easily a rotating crane arm could create an unsettling pendulum effect.[35] Naturalistic conversation with multiple parties would be challenging; Okeanos is also dealing with a fixed point, which means that the onus is on the aerial actor to position himself in relation to Prometheus, rather than having grounded actors manoeuvring to accommodate the flying arrival.[36]

That fixed point of the captive Prometheus is thus set in clear contrast to two different dynamic movements. The first is the rapid (part concerned, part frightened) movement of the chorus, a contrast which continues throughout the play. The second is the flying Okeanos. The contrast between captive and free gods cannot be more starkly posed and lays stress on not only the sufferings of Prometheus, but also the choice the other characters have of what to do with their freedom. The interactions both with the chorus and Okeanos open out the tightly-focused stage action to the broader human and divine background, as in subsequent choral song, particularly those either side of the very still moment of Prometheus' great central speeches on progress and civilisation. The speeches from Prometheus and

Okeanos in the first episode are likewise devoid neither of visual interest nor point.

A different kind of resistance is enacted in the figure of Io, where the similarities and differences to Prometheus are represented through action as well as words. Her switching between recitative, song and speech is similar to the Titan; to have, unusually, two actors' monodies (solo songs) within the same play itself focuses attention on the pair. In contrast to the Titan's stationary endurance, Io's frenzied movement comes in uncontrollable spasms. Her loss of control emphasises the vulnerability of humanity within Zeus' hegemony, and also aligns her with the chorus, whose rapid movement also sets off the Titan's own punishment and emphasises their fear and uncertainty.

The visual development of such contrasts is a key issue in the final scene of the play, with a further double opposition (941-3):

Wait, I see here the lickspittle of Zeus,
the servant of the new ruler.
There's no doubt he's come to report some new tactic.

Hermes' entry is more conventionally flagged, unlike the entrances of Okeanos and Io, who were not 'noticed' in such a way. Prometheus' observation suggests that Hermes is coming up an *eisodos* at 941 rather than flying in on the crane or appearing on the roof. As the play has mostly divine characters, the need to demarcate the divine through the manner of entry is less pressing. There is no mention of flying and for roof (and crane) the same problems of interaction with the bound Prometheus (and chorus) remain. The contrast between the individual Hermes and both the frightened collective of the chorus and the earlier appearances of the somewhat remote Okeanos and the deranged Io is stark. As a confident representative of the power of Zeus, Hermes is full of menace. Unlike Okeanos or Io, he can come close to Prometheus: power is represented through persuasion, threat and control. The violent threats are all the more effective through being delivered by a lone individual; conversely, the direct threat – and Prometheus' resistance – are all the more effective for Prometheus' inability to move. It is, however, not Prometheus who bears the final brunt of Hermes' intervention. At 1058 he turns to threatening the chorus, who respond with their unambiguous statement of solidarity (1063-70). Hermes' final words are to the chorus (1071-9). There is no explicit indication of his departure, but his turn to the chorus suggests he has finished with Prometheus – failing there too, he must leave. The sense of moving towards a conclusion is also conveyed by the change to anapaests from Prometheus' final speech onwards (1040-53).

The final speech from Prometheus (1080-93) describes a cataclysm: earthquake, thunder, lightning, gales and storms, initiating the first stage of Prometheus' long future punishment, predicted by Hermes – a thunderbolt shattering the cliff and burying the Titan (1016-9) for generations (1080-8):

> In deed and not in word,
> the earth has been shattered,
> and a deep echo of thunder
> is growling, and flaming lightning
> balls are shining out, tornadoes are creating
> dust-storms, the blasts of all the
> gales are leaping against each other
> creating a vortex of winds,
> and the sky has been mixed up with the sea;

The likelihood that any of this was staged is remote. Earthquakes are not unknown on the Greek stage – Aeschylus, *Edonoi* fr. 58; Euripides, *Herakles* 904-9, *Erekhtheus* fr. 570.45-54, *Bakkhai* 585-603 – but the technology available was limited. Later references are made to a lightning-machine (*keraunoskopeion*) and a thunder-machine (*bronteion*), but the former, at least, is likely to refer to later, more sophisticated, theatres. Sound effects would be relatively straightforward and easier to implement in the fifth-century theatre, but the case for their existence in the period is not overwhelming.[37] Nor was ancient *skênographia* such as to allow us to contemplate collapsing scenery. Rather, the environmental effects have to be conveyed by word and rhythm alone. If Hermes has left, the performance space is left to the chorus to reinforce the effect with dance that reinforces the stomping anapaestic rhythm.

The remaining performers still need to be removed from the *orkhêstra*. It is usual at the end of Greek tragedy for the performance space to be emptied by characters leaving either with or before the chorus, but it is not clear how either the chorus or Prometheus leave. The chorus have certainly committed to staying with Prometheus until the end, and undoubtedly do so. There is no final choral song or recitative marking their departure. If they leave, it is silent, or something has been lost; *Agamemnon* is similar.[38] Another possibility is that they do not leave conventionally, but are 'buried' with Prometheus, but nothing compels such a staging: Prometheus is nailed up in a cleft, but the chorus are not obviously in such a tight spot; their absence from *Prometheus Unbound* would be difficult to explain if they are buried with Prometheus; and staging is technically considerably simpler if they are not.

Prometheus, meanwhile, has to be buried in some symbolic fashion.[39] There are two main possibilities for this burial and exit.

1. The burial is imagined; the chorus use mimetic dance and posture to indicate Prometheus' burial.[40] If *Prometheus Bound* is followed by *Prometheus Unbound*, then Prometheus could remain bound and notionally buried until the next play.
2. If Prometheus is attached to the central *skênê*, the *ekkyklêma* could be used, even though its regular function is interior scenes. As the most practical means of removing a bound Prometheus it has significant advantages.[41]

All these options would involve unique staging, compared with extant tragedy, but the lack of surviving trilogies makes it difficult to draw comparisons with any confidence. On balance,

I marginally prefer the use of the *ekkyklêma*, but in a trilogy context there are attractions to leaving Prometheus bound across the end of the play.

Crag, world and cosmos

These spectacular effects provide the frame for another conspicuous aspect of the dramaturgy of *Prometheus Bound*, its rendering of plot through extended narratives in speech or song. Some of the speeches I have discussed already: Prometheus' account of the divine back-story (Chapter 2) and human progress (Chapter 3). As well as providing story elements through flash-backs and flash-forwards, these serve to expand the play's scope chronologically and metaphysically, from the wars of divine succession to the latest stages of human civilisation.

Although the chorus are primarily reactive, their emotional response also expands *Prometheus Bound*'s frame of reference. Their explanation of their arrival describes them listening in the depths of the ocean (133-5). The whole human world (406-30) and all the seas and rivers (431-5) are distressed by Prometheus' pain.[42] They contrast Prometheus' present misfortunes with the happy day of his marriage to Hesione, their sister (553-60). Just as, then, the pinioned Prometheus provides a fixed point around which his interlocutors revolve, so too the scenes at the crag are extended in cosmic terms through these extended narratives. Such a use of spoken and sung narrative is used by Aeschylus elsewhere, not least in the equally 'static' *Persians* and *Seven*, and even in the *Suppliant Women*, albeit with less chronological and cosmic sweep.

The human scope of *Prometheus Bound* is particularly developed in the Io scene, in Prometheus' account of her descendants and especially his narrative of her future and past travels. He gives an account of the Eastern world, in a series of arcs, from the Caucasus round to the boundary between Europe and Asia (700-41), thence down to Ethiopia and back up to Egypt (786-98), and finally from Greece into the Balkans (827-41). In its geographical scope, its mix of the historical, semi-mythical and mythical races, and its imprecise and lacunose nature, it gives a good impression of mid-fifth-century ethnography and geography, an impression furthered by the aetiologies that explain modern names for geographic features.

The last narrative, of Io's earliest travels, is the clearest: Prometheus takes up the narration from Molossia (in Thessaly) across to Dodona, in Epirus (north-west Greece), where the famous oracle spoke to her. Then she went up the Adriatic coast ('Gulf of Rhea') before her wandering reverses course (838), i.e. heads east to reach Prometheus' crag. Her journey up the coast is the explanation, Prometheus says, of the name Ionian Sea.

The location of Prometheus' crag is itself slightly vague, a remote part of 'Skythia' (2), an elastic place that can encompass vaguely any part north and east of Thrace, or the entire Eurasian steppe, but more specifically that part between the Danube to the Don.[43] Plausible mountains on the steppe are rare; given that Io will travel east to skirt the Skythians, it is best to imagine Prometheus attached to a version of the Carpathians, or else an entirely imaginary northern range. He is clearly not attached to the Caucasus, an ancient misunderstanding, pointed out by the *Life of Aeschylus*.[44]

From Prometheus' crag, Io will head east, skirting on the seaward side Skythian nomads (who live in wagons and are horse-riding archers, 707-11). Either a northerly route beside the ocean, or southerly along the Black Sea can be construed.[45] She then keeps the iron-working Khalybians on the left, before heading up the river Hybristes (the 'violent river', not otherwise known), crossing the Caucasus (here displaced to the north of the Black Sea) and heading south (722) to the Amazons. In contrast to the Skythians (and Khalybians) who are not hospitable, the Amazons 'who hate men' (724) will welcome Io (728) – as she is a woman oppressed by male sexuality. Thence Io should proceed to the Cimmerian Bosporus (the Straits of Kerč), which connects the Black Sea and the Maeotian Lake (Sea of Azov), one of the tradiitonal boundaries between Europe and Asia. Crossing over, Io will enter Asia.

The Bosporus ('cow-strait') is another aetiology (732-4), while care is also taken to reconcile two variant accounts of the Amazons. A location between Dnieper and Don fits with one Greek tradition, but a variant that places them south of the Black Sea is explained as due to a migration (724-7).[46] The Khalybians are usually south of the Black Sea, but Io is still conceived of as in Europe at this stage, so *Prometheus Bound* is following (or may be the source for) the minority view that puts them in Skythia.[47]

The Asian leg enters more fantastic domains. Crossing the Bosporus, Prometheus tells Io to go east to the plain of Kisthene (793), where the Gorgons live (793, 798-800) and the three Phorkides, daughters of Phorkys or Graiai, who share one tooth and one eye (794-7). Traditionally, both sets of sisters live by the ocean, but the Gorgons in the far west not the far east. At least one contemporary interpreted Kisthene as the ends of the earth, the comic poet Kratinos, and that remoteness is suggested also by these monsters never seeing the sun or the moon (706-7).[48] Other threats in the far east are griffins (803-4) and the Arimaspians, described as a mounted horde of one-eyed men. This section owes something to the *Arimaspeia*, an ethnographic poem of perhaps the seventh century BCE by the shadowy Aristeas of Prokonnesos. Aristeas apparently, however, located the Arimaspians, in the far north, not the far east, and no other version puts them explicitly on horses.[49] They are said here to be based around a gold-bearing river, Plouton ('River Wealth'), which like its cousin Hybristes in the north is likely to be an invention with a pointed name.

Io will come to the deep south, Ethiopia ('far-off', 807), essentially everything south of Egypt, extending to the far south east of the circular world. Following the river 'Aithiops', Io will come to the papyrus hills (811), from which the Nile flows (812). This seems to mean the First Cataract, below Elephantine (*katabasmos*, 811; usually *Katadoupoi* (or *-pa*) in Greek, cf. Herodotos 2.17). The Nile leads to the delta (813-4), her final destination. When Prometheus resumes the narrative at 844-52, he mentions the city of Canopus (846-7) at the north-west of the delta, mentioned also in *Suppliant Women* 311.

Egypt had been a source of fascination for the Greeks since the beginning of its poetic traditions. Io's establishment of an *apoikia* (colony) there suggests long-established Greek settlements, such as the trading post at Naukratis.[50] Egypt featured strongly in the geography of Hekataios (late sixth or early fifth century), against which Herodotos' account is explicitly targeted.[51] It appears as a source of both the fantastic and fascination in Aeschylus' *Suppliant Women* long before it plays a similar role in Herodotos and, in a different way, Plato.

The ethnographic interest displayed in these passages, the insistence on aetiology and contemporary terminology, the concern to weigh up differing traditions, and the mix of fantastic, legendary and more securely attested cultures and topography all situate these speeches in the mainstream of fifth-century ethnography and geography, which is a further element in the intellectual developments that I sketched in Chapter 3. There is no single source for the accounts here, but the fantastic elements reflect an earlier strand than the more historically plausible ethnography of Herodotos (who is associated, like Protagoras, with Thourioi, but whose work is not attested in Athens earlier than 425[52]) and like other aspects of the intellectual context suggests that *Prometheus Bound* sits in the earlier part of its chronological window. The clear effect of these narratives is to expand the frame of reference of *Prometheus Bound*, to encompass the world in its geographical and cultural scope, while remaining dramaturgically anchored to the cliff. This is continued in *Prometheus Unbound*, as Herakles ventures westwards. The aetiologies and references to contemporary disputes bridge the chronological divide, as the narrative sustains the twin focus of Prometheus' northern crag and contemporary Athens.

The theatre of violence

The most striking and shocking aspect of *Prometheus Bound*, however, is the sheer amount of physical violence depicted on stage. It is not, of course, that displays of madness, physical torment or death are unknown to Greek tragedy – in addition to Ajax's suicide, examples include the broken Hippolytos in Euripides' (*Hippolytos* 1347-1461, Herakles dying from the poisoned robe in Sophokles' *Trakhiniai* 983-1274, or Orestes' madness in both Aeschylus' *Libation Bearers* 1047-62 and, extremely floridly, in Euripides' *Orestes* (especially 211-315). What is different in *Prometheus Bound* is the amount of physical and mental pain, for both Prometheus and Io, its duration, from the first scene to last, and the manner of its presentation.

In Aristotle's account of Greek tragedy, physical manifestations of pain are not central to Greek tragedy. The stirring of pity and fear in the audience follows primarily from plot, from reversal of circumstances, and particularly a character's awareness of such a change in fortune. It does not come from the shudder as a spike is driven through flesh or the presentation of unqualified madness. While Prometheus is aware of the reversal of his fortune and the ironies of being unable to save himself (in the short term), such recognition plays a very subordinate role to his physical suffering, and the question of whether he has in fact made any mistake (*hamartia*) is a point of ongoing contention between him and Zeus (see especially 266). Io, meanwhile, is the victim of a will that is both capricious and unmotivated by anything other than lust. Pity, fear and related emotions thus come from a more elemental level in *Prometheus Bound*. The play poses a question that can sometimes be felt hovering uncomfortably around Greek tragedy: does tragic pleasure arise out of the enjoyment of others' suffering? Is Greek tragedy on some level about the pornography of violence and suffering?

Prometheus Bound foregrounds the audience's own actions in watching pain. Hephaistos describes Prometheus' isolation as being hidden from view (21-2) and disagrees with Kratos about the nature of the spectacle (69-70):

Heph. You are looking at a spectacle that is a painful sight to the eyes.
Krat. I see him getting his just deserts.

Prometheus likewise emphasises his appearance. Left by Hephaistos, Kratos and Bia, he calls on the elements (including 'the sun that sees all', 91) to watch his sufferings (92-3). The opening sequence for each visitor, bar the last, Hermes, highlights the visual spectacle, as Prometheus invites his visitors to look at him and his punishment. When he hears the chorus arriving, he wonders whether they have come to watch him, using the term appropriate for someone visiting a festival (*theôros*, 118). He calls on them to look at his suffering (119); in their epirrhematic exchange, the double invitation to see and observe (141) is returned by the chorus (143-8); he returns to the theme at the end of his long speech setting out the backstory (238, 241, 246). Likewise, he asks whether Okeanos has come to watch (*epoptês*, 'as spectator', 299; *theôrêsôn*, 'to watch', 302; *derkou*, 'see', 304) the spectacle (*theama*, 304), to which, again, Okeanos responds (307). At her entrance, Io demands to know who she is seeing (561), a question ultimately answered after her descent into madness (itself featuring hallucinations, 569, cf. 553) and she is answered eventually at 612. Prometheus' final words echo his first: 'you see how I am suffering what is beyond justice' (1093).

Central to all these instances is audience response. Prometheus fears that the sight of him will afford the gods pleasure (155-9), a possibility denied by the chorus, excepting only Zeus (160-2). He also uses it as a basis to attack Zeus' reputation (*kleos*, 241). Pity underpins the chorus' response both to the sight of Prometheus (143-8, 244-5, 540) and to Io (*dystheata*, 'difficult to watch', 690, 695, 894-900). Pity is central, too, to Prometheus' description of his own sufferings (238) and his sight of Typhos (352), but it is conspicuously absent from the roving eye of Zeus (earlier on Io, 654; more generally, 904) and the surveillance of Argos (568-9, 678-9). The emphasis on the act of viewing, the object of viewing and on emotional response in the viewer all encourage the audience (spectators, *theatai*) to reflect upon their own actions, at no moment more than the opening and closing words of Prometheus, when the only addressee is his general environment.

Imagery associated with sight is far from alien to Greek tragedy, not least in plays such as Sophokles' *Ajax* or *Oedipus Tyrannus*, where sight and insight are closely intertwined.[53] *Prometheus Bound* too uses similar language, not least in relation to human progress (see, for example, 447, 547, 843). Where *Prometheus Bound* differs is in the emphasis on the quality of the spectacle of one character, which is unusually extensive and blunt. The two strands come together in the Hermes scene. In the opening exchange, Prometheus does not emphasise his own spectacle – indeed, Hermes is the only character who Prometheus himself identifies by sight before they have spoken (941). Their dialogue emphasises not pity (or even mockery) but whether Prometheus will learn from his painful experiences, which are figured visually (951, 997; compare the chorus at 553 [Prometheus] and 894-900 [Io]); Prometheus counters with foresight (998) and what he claims he will see in the future (Zeus' fall, 958). Hermes claims, moreover, to have a different impression (*eoikas* 971) of Prometheus' motivation and interactions (971-3):

Herm.   You look to me like you are luxuriating in your
        current situation.
Prom.   Luxuriating? I wish I could see my enemies
        luxuriating like this. And I mean you among them.

Prometheus here interprets Hermes as thinking specifically of his visual appearance.[54] His comments are – justifiably – bitter, but also display a concern for directing the reception of his own spectacle.[55] This sense of self-staging is amplified by the claim that his actions were in full knowledge of the consequences, including the suffering that he will undergo (101-4). Hermes is, of course, exaggerating when he suggests that Prometheus is enjoying it in some kind of self-indulgent or narcissistic way; but there is a sense nonetheless that this is a self-conscious political stunt.

When Aristophanes comes to parody *Prometheus Bound*, this element of vision and spectacle is inverted. Prometheus' concern for how audiences take his spectacle is turned into the absurd spectacle of him avoiding onlookers. In *Birds* 1494-1552, he comes in swaddled up, in an attempt to evade Zeus' vision, gives Peisetairos a parasol to hold over them while they are talking, reveals to mortals how to displace the gods and gain all Zeus' political arts, and then heads off with said parasol, masquerading as the Panathenaic procession. That Aristophanes has *Prometheus Bound* in mind is made clear by 1547: 'I hate all the gods, as you know' (cf. *Prometheus Bound* 975).[56] The Titan, proud and careful of his appearance, here ends up looking supremely silly.

Gesture politics

The spectacle of *Prometheus Bound* is bold, imaginative and undeniably grand, but it is far from empty. Rather, the staging serves both to amplify the cosmic nature of the story, to connect the divine level of representation to both its human participants (Io) and the extra-fictional onlookers (the audience), to put an unprecedented focus on the sufferings of one character, who becomes the pivot for the action that is represented visually on stage and narrated off stage, and to lead the audience to confront the effects of watching that unprecedented sacrifice and suffering. There is an attempt here both to address pity (and, indeed, fear) at a raw physical level and to connect the physicality of suffering with the elemental and philosophical issues at the heart of the play. This kind of grandstanding, the unashamed drama of political, theatrical and religious provocation, may not be to everyone's taste – certainly the passion of Prometheus is as far from Aristotelian prescriptions as it is from modern black-box theatre – but it provides an arresting and challenging performance. The interplay of characters, sympathetic and hostile, crude and sophisticated, affords a variety of perspectives on the central focus. They suggest that this particular political activist can be, perhaps necessarily, harsh, demanding, unfair, single-minded, wilful – even that he may be relishing being the centre of attention just that little too much.

Both the heroic qualities and the question marks over Prometheus will be exploited in the rich and creative reception of *Prometheus Bound*, a reception which, more than classical critics, relishes its ideological, visual and auditory agitation.

5

The Radical Tradition

The reception of *Prometheus Bound* is closely intertwined with that of radical and progressive thought. Its themes of political rebellion and technological and social progress have not always endeared it to readers, but it has been a talismanic text from the late eighteenth century onwards. Radical thinkers have returned repeatedly to *Prometheus Bound* and its problematic allegories in order to think through these central ideas and have created a series of commentaries on the Aeschylean text and its reception, and how classical antiquity itself relates to progress and participation.

The play's very earliest reception has already been touched upon in discussing the question of authenticity. The importance of *Prometheus Bound* or its trilogy in classical receptions of Prometheus is muted. Notable exceptions are Cicero's adaptation of *Prometheus Unbound* to make a Stoic argument (*Tusculan Disputations* 2.23-5), perhaps Varro's Menippean Satire, *Prometheus Liber* (*Free Prometheus*) and Lucian's versions of Prometheus: the dialogue between Prometheus and Hermes at the former's crucifixion in Lucian's *Prometheus* may owe something to *Prometheus Bound*, although other strands are paramount; Prometheus' warning to Zeus in his pursuit of Thetis in *Dialogues of the Gods* 5 seems closer to Aeschylus and the plot of *Prometheus Unbound*.[1] In addition to the Hesiodic and Platonic versions, the strand that becomes dominant in ancient, medieval and Renaissance contexts is that where Prometheus creates man from mud.[2] This version was clearly circulating as early as the late fourth or early third century

BCE,[3] but the version by Ovid was particularly important for later receptions (*Metamorphoses* 1.82-6[4]):

> The son of Iapetos moulded the mud, mixed with
>   rain-water,
> into the shape of the gods who control everything,
> and whereas all other animals look face-down at the
>   ground,
> he gave mankind a head held high and instructed him to
>   see the sky
> and to lift up his face and raise it to the stars.

The story and iconography of this version became assimilated to Christian narratives and iconography. Medieval texts continue euhemeristic (rationalising and allegorical) approaches from late antiquity: Prometheus rationalised as a historical inventor (of sculpture, rings, astrology, etc.), or Promethean fire as the human soul and Prometheus as divine providence (Plotinus); and Prometheus' tortures allegorised as the cares of the world (Fulgentius). In Renaissance and Humanist texts, Prometheus is allegorised as the *homo sapiens* (wise man) or *homo doctus* (learned man) who leads brute man (*homo naturalis*) into civilisation (*homo civilis*), viewed either optimistically (Boccaccio, Erasmus) or pessimistically (Ficino). In more popular iconography, such as emblem books, Prometheus is allegorised as the proud over-achiever.[5]

Meanwhile, *Prometheus Bound* formed one of the Byzantine 'triad' of Aeschylean plays, preserved for the school curriculum. The rediscovery of Greek tragedy in the West was gradual. The first print edition of Aeschylus was in 1518 at the Aldine Press, edited by Asulanus (Giovanni Francesco Torresano d'Asola); an edition of *Prometheus* was published in 1548 by Auratus (Jean Dorat) at Paris; more important editions were those of 1552 by Turnebus at Paris and Robertello at Venice, and in 1557 by Victorius (Pietro Vettori) with contributions by Stephanus (Henri Estienne). Latin translations, somewhat later than those of Sophokles and Euripides, were published by J. San-

ravius in 1555 and Mathias Garbitius (Matija Grbic) in 1559 at
Basel.[6] Some isolated influences can be seen in Italian art of the
sixteenth century[7] and a school performance in the original
Greek (somewhat augmented) is also known from Strasbourg in
July 1609.[8] Access to the play for English writers would have
been either in Greek or in a Latin translation until the second
half of the eighteenth century, when vernacular translations
appeared; even in those limited terms it was the edition of
Thomas Stanley (London, 1663, and much reprinted for almost
two centuries) that made Aeschylus particularly accessible. The
influence of *Prometheus Bound* up to at least the mid-seven-
teenth century was thus necessarily limited. Even in
adventurous and progressive thinkers such as Francis Bacon,
the medieval traditions of Prometheus are still very strong, as
in his *de sapientia veterum* (*On the Wisdom of the Ancients*) 16,
which figures Prometheus and progress as divine providence.[9]

Milton and the rediscovery of Aeschylus

The pivotal figure in the English-language reception of
Prometheus is John Milton. The Titan is a thread in his three
major late poems: *Paradise Lost* (first ten-volume edition, 1667;
second twelve-volume edition, 1674), *Paradise Regained* and
Samson Agonistes (both published 1671).[10] Milton had been
interested in the figure of Prometheus since university and was
also, unusually for the period, an admirer of Aeschylus.[11]
Prometheus Bound influences these poems in plots, character,
and, arguably, specific borrowings.[12] Milton, in turn, was central to *Prometheus Bound*'s later reception, particularly by the
Romantics, who read and rewrote Milton in Promethean terms.
Milton, however, challenges Aeschylus with a pessimistic interpretation of Prometheus.

Aeschylus presents an extreme provocation over the fall of
man. Whereas Milton is interested in explaining the fall and
remedying its problems, Aeschylus seems to be asking, 'What
problem?' Milton confronts the Aeschylean myth head-on with
the Edenic myth[13] and exploits ambiguities in the Aeschylean

Prometheus for the character of Satan in *Paradise Lost*. Satan, like Prometheus, challenges divine authority after working closely with it, is cast out of heaven and is imprisoned (*Paradise Lost* 1.44-9 [cf. *Prometheus Bound* 6, 1016-19]):

Him the Almighty Power
Hurled headlong flaming from th' ethereal sky
With hideous ruin and combustion down
To bottomless perdition, there to dwell
In adamantine chains and penal fire,
Who durst defy th' Omnipotent to arms.

Both affirm that they will endure any and all tortures that their all-powerful adversary can inflict upon them (I.94-9; cf. Chapter 2). As the Romantics recognised, however, making Satan a Promethean character is a risky strategy. Blake famously claimed Milton for the devil's party.[14] Satan indeed has attractions, espousing freedom and an opposition to tyranny. Like Prometheus, he dominates his poem and there is a strong temptation to focalise through him. His character, however, is complex – and here Blake's claim weakens. For Satan is courageous, strong-willed and defiant, but also arrogant and proud, convinced of his own destiny. In this he is both like and unlike Prometheus. His pride is much more explicit, but there is still a personal element in Prometheus' challenge to Zeus. Both seek revenge: for Satan, 'spite … with spite is best repaid' (*Paradise Lost* IX.178); for Prometheus, 'we should hurt the ones who hurt us' (970). As a reading of *Prometheus Bound*, *Paradise Lost* raises questions about the motivation of Aeschylus' protagonist.

Politically, Blake's claim points to a faultline in Milton's work. Milton, who had very publicly defended regicide (and was thus in great personal peril at the Restoration),[15] is writing against the rebel Satan and in defence of the divine king. That apparent contradiction might be tackled by maintaining a strong distinction between human and divine monarchy, but Milton is also writing in the context of the explosion of radical thought during the English Revolution, where the allegorical use of religious or other myths was widely used and understood and would be highly suggestive.[16] Neither the political context nor Milton's own political activities, however, allow a straightforward interpretation of individual liberty against political authority. *Paradise Lost* was written for the most part during and after the failure of the Commonwealth (for which Milton had been pamphleteer, propagandist and functionary) and the return to monarchy. It is possible to read *Paradise Lost* in that context as a taxonomy of revolutionary failure: disunity, lack of resolution and ill-discipline are characteristics of Satan's forces, suggestive, perhaps, of religious and political contemporaries. The poem raises the questions over the extent and application of liberty.

The questioning of the idealism of *Prometheus Bound* can also be seen in the position of humanity: Satan sees the very existence of humans as an affront to his kind. His personal spite results in the corruption of Eve and Adam, in stark contrast to the Titan's rescue of the human race from oblivion. Just as Aeschylus inverted the Hesiodic myth of decline, so too Milton reclaims the Prometheus myth for the pessimists by reintroducing Hesiod. Satan's corruption is the direct analogue of the Hesiodic fall (*Paradise Lost* IV.714-9):

> More lovely than Pandora, whom the gods
> Endowed with all their gifts, and O too like
> In sad event, when to the unwiser son
> Of Japhet brought by Hermes, she ensnared
> Mankind with her fair looks, to be avenged
> On him who had stole Jove's authentic fire.

Eve and Adam are compared to Pandora and Epimetheus, but the balance of responsibility for the fall shifts from the divine to the human level, and from masculine to feminine. Humans unwittingly emulate Lucifer's own earlier Promethean act of rebellion.[17] Contrast *Prometheus Bound*, where the sole human, Io, suffers, like Prometheus, the abusive power of the gods and struggles to resist.

In his other late works, Milton again addresses questions of freedom, authority and revolutionary leadership. In *Samson Agonistes*, the Promethean role of humanity is more explicit and optimistic, co-opted for a redemptive vision. Both the dramatic situation and the literary form all suggest Aeschylus' play very strongly. Milton's preface (54-61) itself invites us to read the play against the three Greek tragedians.[18]

The action is set around the central character, Samson, who is a captive of the Philistines, blinded, chained and exploited as slave labour, an outcast from his own people. He recalls both the captive Prometheus and the blinded and humbled Oedipus of Sophokles' *Oedipus at Kolonos*.[19] The play develops, like *Prometheus Bound*, as a series of dialogues between the protagonist and interlocutors. These aim variously to comfort him (the chorus) and/or to engineer his release. His father, Manoa, aims to ransom him from the Philistines, while his erstwhile wife Dalila seeks forgiveness and/or resumption of marriage. Taunts come from the Philistine champion, Harapha, and Officers sent from the Philistine nobles. Samson remains adamant that he will remain a prisoner. The chorus' intervention recalls the Okeanids and to a certain extent Okeanos, but the conciliatory older man is developed particularly in Manoa.[20] The various Philistines, and Dalila, take on elements of Hermes. There is no place for an Io role. Rather, woman continues as temptress, serving the enemy. As in *Prometheus Bound*, the dialogues reveal the back-story and enlarge the scope of the play to the wider political and geographical context. They also project the play forward in time, and reflect on the fate and role of humanity.

Like Prometheus, Samson exhibits defiance and single-mindedness, but shows more despair at his double servitude – prison and blindness. He demonstrates clearer self-recognition than Prometheus, that pride led him to over-reach himself – not so much in his rebellion against his leaders, who had been reaching accommodation with the Philistines, but his insistence on marriage to Dalila, which laid him open to temptation and loss of power (hair). Promethean defiance is here presented in a more ethical context, and opens up potential for reflection, moral development and ultimately redemption. The shift from Titan or fallen angel towards a human protagonist also creates an allegory closer to its audience. Like *Prometheus Bound*, *Samson Agonistes* ends in the burial of the central figure, but Prometheus' proud theatricality (see Chapter 4) here becomes a denial of spectacle: Samson's final show is to take place in the theatre of the Philistines. He recovers his resolve and, when it looks as if he has given in to the Philistines, brings down the house on them.

In the closing books of *Paradise Lost*, Adam and Eve repent and the Archangel Michael consoles them with an overview of mankind up to the Second Coming, but *Samson Agonistes* presents a much clearer idea of the way human development ought to go. In particular, unhindered liberty and pride need tempering with humility, faith and repentance, and in some sense submission ('What will they then / But force the Spirit of grace itself, and bind / His consort Liberty.' *Paradise Lost* XII.524-6). This moral and spiritual theme reaches its fullest expression in *Paradise Regained*, with the ultimate example, the Son of Man.

Samson Agonistes exploits tensions in *Prometheus Bound* to reinstate the distance between god and man, which *Prometheus Bound* undermines with its emphasis on autonomous human development. That materialist theme is also addressed in Milton's poems. Wisdom and technology are problematic, and like intellectual (and political) freedom require tempering and moderation. Knowledge '... Oppresses else with surfeit, and soon turns / Wisdom to folly, as nourishment to wind' (*Paradise Lost* VII.129-30).[21] Clearly, however, there is a great ambivalence here – Milton's works are infused with Classical learning at every level. Milton confronts the problem head-on in *Paradise Regained*. Athens is represented as deeply problematic and education itself as questionable. Satan's last attempt to tempt the Son of God is to set before him the resources of learning with which to refute his opponents. The pinnacle of these are Classical sources – philosophy, drama (especially IV.261-5), poetry, rhetoric. Athens stands for the classical world as a whole. Christ's response rejects the dependence upon classical ideas, especially those promoting materialism and scepticism about the divine order and the fall, and discussing the nature of civil government. Christian law, mythology and art are promoted in its stead (*Paradise Regained* IV.334-8, 356-64) and above all the spirit and judgement that they inculcate (*Paradise Regained* IV.322-6):

> ... who reads
> Incessantly, and to his reading brings not
> A spirit and judgment equal or superior
> (And what he brings, what needs he elsewhere seek?),
> Uncertain and unsettled still remains ...

Milton's reworking of Prometheus thus exploits tensions in the fifth-century representation, and introduces a broader moral dimension. Prometheus' emphasis on his heroism is queried and the allegorical move from Titan to human is challenged. Conversely, Milton's own narratives may not evade the implications of *Prometheus Bound*. The attempt to close down excessive freedom is problematic, given the powerful espousal of liberty by the protagonists of both *Paradise Lost* and *Samson Agonistes*. Fundamentally, the logic of the fall and the logic of materialist advancement are incompatible. Freedom to know and freedom to participate are here intimately bound up. Milton accepts the idea – embodied in *Prometheus Bound* and his representation of Classical Athens – that intellectual curiosity is a corollary of that 'fierce democraty' (*Paradise Regained* IV.269). In the final reckoning, he opts for limits to both – ultimately, it is the elect who will survive, guaranteed by God and Faith.

Romantic heroism

Aeschylus in general and *Prometheus Bound* in particular did not appeal to neo-classical tastes. As an example, he fared particularly badly in Père Brumoy's anthology/summary of

Greek drama, *Le Théâtre des grecs* (*The Theatre of the Greeks*, 1730; translated into English in 1759[22]). No play was translated complete, the works were evidently baffling to him, and *Prometheus Bound* most of all (described as 'monstrous'). The point was noted by his English translator, Charlotte Lennox. Over the course of the eighteenth century Prometheus was re-evaluated and Aeschylean drama became much more widely accessible, as he was translated into vernacular languages: Italian in 1754 (M. Cesarotti at Padua; M.A. Giacomelli at Rome), French in 1770 (J.-J. Le France de Pompignan, Paris) and 1785-9 (F.J.G. de la Porte du Theil, in the second edition of Brumoy), English in 1777. *Prometheus Bound* was the first Aeschylean play to be translated into English, by Thomas Morell in 1773, anticipating Robert Potter's complete translation by four years.[23] Prometheus, meanwhile, was undergoing a rehabilitation, which progressively reshaped the (over-reaching) Prometheus-creator myth into that of Prometheus the poetic creator from Shaftesbury (Anthony Ashley Cooper, 3rd Earl of Shaftesbury) to Goethe.[24] Goethe made four attempts at adapting the Prometheus myth – an unfinished play of 1773, of which two acts survive; a poem *Prometheus*, reworking parts of that drama (1774; published unofficially in 1785; published by Goethe in 1789); a translation of *Prometheus Bound*, which was abandoned; and a Pandora play (1810).[25] Goethe's *Prometheus* poem is in many respects the Prometheus of Enlightenment values,[26] but aspects are reminiscent of *Prometheus Bound*: the challenge to Zeus is undeniably there, as the poem explores human emancipation from the divine; Prometheus is aligned with mankind and against the gods in the use of sympathy and pity (27, 37-41) and, more generally, emotion. Zeus is likened to a thoughtless and destructive boy. The context is ostensibly pagan, but there are strong hints too of a challenge to Christian assumptions (21, adapting I Corinthians 13.11). The heroic (and angry) individualism was a central feature of the Sturm und Drang movement and subsequent German Romanticism. Goethe's poem was set a number of times in the Romantic period, not least by Schubert (1819, D.674) and Wolf (1889). In other Romantic and post-Romantic music, Prometheus was also subject of a ballet by Beethoven (*The Creatures of Prometheus*, op. 43, 1801), a symphonic poem by Liszt (1855), setting Herder's *Prometheus Unbound* (a continuation of Aeschylus), an opera, *Prométhée*, by Fauré (1900) and Scriabin's *Prometheus: Poem of Fire*, op. 60 (1910).[27]

In the nineteenth century, Aeschylus became a key figure for the Romantics, celebrated by figures such as A.W. Schlegel and Victor Hugo, the latter comparing him to Shakespeare.[28] In England, the Romantics took up the Promethean challenge posed by Milton. Blake's appropriation and reinterpretation of Satan was one tactic; another was to return explicitly to Prometheus. *Prometheus Bound* was a significant text for (at least) Byron, Blake and the Shelleys. Byron composed a version of the second stasimon of the play while still at school (1804), and Prometheus became an important symbol in his poetry, including his *Ode to Napoleon*, and lies behind many of his heroic figures. In 1816, he composed a poem, *Prometheus*, most directly influenced by *Prometheus Bound*, which Shelley translated for him during their stay in Switzerland.[29] The bound Prometheus, in particular, symbolises for Byron the state of humanity, divine and not-divine, and the struggle and striving of human existence.

The Titans, Prometheus included, lie behind a great deal of Blake's mythology and iconography, particularly his touchstone figure of Orc.[30] They also influence the visual work of many contemporaries.[31] A striking instance of Romantic iconography is the slightly later 'Prometheus Bound' by Thomas Cole (1840), one of the Hudson River group of artists in the USA.[32]

The most explicit and influential development of *Prometheus Bound* was in Percy Shelley's *Prometheus Unbound*.[33] Shelley foregrounds the problem posed by Satan, and sets Aeschylus against Milton (preface):

Prometheus is, in my judgement, a more poetical character than Satan, because, in addition to courage and majesty and firm and patient opposition to omnipotent force, he is susceptible of being described as exempt from the taints of ambition, envy, revenge, and a desire for personal aggrandisement, which in the Hero of Paradise Lost, interferes with the interest.[34]

A second problem that Shelley saw was that *Prometheus Bound* results in a stalemate: neither Zeus nor Titan (nor Hermes) are budging from their position. How could resolution be achieved if Prometheus were not somehow to back down? I discussed some possible outcomes in Chapter 2. Shelley's solution was to develop the moral and spiritual angle taken by Milton. Shelley introduces the concept of love, which reorientates the confrontation towards harmony and reconciliation.

Shelley adds to the Aeschylean myth a curse on Jupiter, which facilitates a dramatic shift of Prometheus away from hate. In the first act, Prometheus repents of this curse, and frees Jupiter from his torment (*Prometheus Unbound* I.292-305):

Phantom of Jupiter.
  ... Heap on thy soul by virtue of this Curse
  Ill deeds, then be thou damned, beholding good,
  Both infinite as is the Universe,
  And thou, and thy self-torturing solitude.
  An awful image of calm power
  Though now thou sittest, let the hour
  Come, when thou must appear to be
  That which thou art internally.
  And after many a false and fruitless crime
  Scorn track thy lagging fall through boundless space
    and time.
Prometheus.
  Were those my words, O Parent?
The Earth.
  They were thine.
Prometheus.
  It doth repent me: words are quick and vain;

> Grief for awhile is blind, and so was mine.
> I wish no living thing to suffer pain.

Although Jupiter continues to torture Prometheus via the Furies, orchestrated by Mercury, and still demands to know the circumstances of his downfall (for Prometheus refuses to reveal that), the hate and spite is no longer mutual. Prometheus is now only pain incarnate (I.477-8).

Shelley reunites Milton's privileged Christian values with Promethean liberty by removing the patriarchal God, reinstating Jupiter as tyrant and reinterpreting Christ as a secularised hero of suffering and love (I.584-602). Prometheus' ultimate despair is the persecution of Christ-like figures in the name of Christ himself (603-631), which is representative of the trough into which humanity had sunk: justice and goodness are despised, humans are beset by terror, not least terror about knowledge, and, above all, bereft of Promethean love and empathy. Jupiter's regime is evil not only in itself, but because it has sapped human will.

Prometheus' turn towards love is the precondition for the removal of Jupiter's tyranny. Demogorgon, a minor figure in *Paradise Lost*, is here promoted into the figure that takes Jupiter from his throne. He is the son greater than the father, described by Prometheus at *Prometheus Bound* 768 (cf. 958-9), and draws on the Hesiodic Typhoeus (*Theogony* 820-80) and Aeschylean Typhos (351-72). *Prometheus Unbound* III.i.51-8:

> Jupiter
> ... Awful shape, what art thou? Speak!
> Demogorgon
> Eternity – demand no direr name.
> Descend, and follow me down the abyss;
> I am thy child, as thou wert Saturn's child.
> Mightier than thee; and we must dwell together
> Henceforth in darkness. – Lift thy lightnings not.
> The tyranny of Heaven none may retain,
> Or reassume, or hold succeeding thee ...

116

Demogorgon is a rather shady character, and not only for owing his literary existence to a scribal slip of the pen.[35] He is located in Hell, but in his encounter with the Oceanid Asia (II.iv), he is presented as standing somewhat aside from the logic of divine succession. Drawing on the Hesiodic myths, Asia presents the succession and time itself as subsequent to Heaven, Earth, Light and Love (II.iv.32-3). Again, Demogorgon reveals that although all things are subject to time and chance, Love remains prior (119-120). He reveals that Jupiter is slave as well as tyrant. Unlike Prometheus but like current humanity, Jupiter is slave to his fears.

Given the priority of love, Prometheus' act of repentance has the means both to undo Jupiter and to unravel the logic of power and tyranny. Demogorgon's removal of Jupiter supersedes the idea of succession and allows love to become transcendent.[36] The rest of the poem explores the replacement of discord with harmony. *Prometheus Unbound* III.iii.34-9:

> Prometheus.
> ... And we will search, with looks and words of love
> For hidden thoughts each lovelier than the last,
> Our unexhausted spirits, and like lutes
> Touched by the skill of the enamoured wind,
> Weave harmonies divine, yet ever new,
> From difference sweet where discord cannot be.

A removal of strife and the return to the Golden Age is both anti-Hesiodic and anti-Aeschylean. Prometheus is still responsible for speech, knowledge, crafts and science (II.iv.74-9). Shelley shares the Aeschylean critique of human ignorance, but diverges from Aeschylus on human development. The future in *Prometheus Bound* is optimistic – knowledge and hope are human goods – but not idealising, in contrast to Shelley's reinstated Golden Age. Shelley's future embraces diversity and difference, but without the taint of discord. The metaphor is musical: difference and harmony. The lessons of science by themselves are not enough – poetry and music are all higher expressions of human will. After all, as Shelley was to argue in *A Defence of Poetry*, the poets are the true legislators.

Prometheus enables the human turn to love, but he is also an allegory of human potential in this respect, just as Jupiter symbolises the negative potential of the human will, that tends towards evil and tyranny. The poem is a clarion-call to resist tyranny and, especially in its closing act, a celebration of the human (rather than holy) spirit. Its presentation of non-violent freedom and diversity is certainly attractive, but anxieties remain. If Milton is waiting for the external agency to stand guarantor for the New World Order, Shelley is suggesting that the solution comes from within. And yet the mystery of Demogorgon is an obfuscation of causation that is perhaps too convenient.

The situation of the entire poem, with the partial exception of Herakles, on the divine plane universalises and idealises, but here the distance from material human experience is palpable. For all that Shelley himself was a radical activist, his allegorical stance in *Prometheus Unbound*, with its emphasis on abstraction and internal reflection, lacks the immediacy of the Aeschylean play, whose myth is more firmly rooted and more concrete. Although Shelley poses the question whether rationalism by itself is enough for a fully free state, the emphasis on the moral and spiritual dimension also serves to abstract the myth away from the specific material and political implications of technology.

The creation of science fiction

Percy Shelley eschewed material discussion in favour of an idealised potential future. Mary Shelley, by contrast, opened up a whole new terrain of investigation with her scrutiny of the myth of rationalism and technological progress in her novel *Frankenstein: or the Modern Prometheus* (1818; substantially revised for the third edition of 1831). This book has dominated subsequent interpretations of the Prometheus myth, in the return to technology and industrialisation and in scepticism about naïve utopianism.

Prometheanism in the novel is most obviously attached to the eponymous Victor Frankenstein, whose creation of life echoes the myth of Prometheus-creator. *Frankenstein* roots *Prometheus Bound*'s myth of progress firmly in the lab, but both lab and creator are slightly peculiar.[37] Victor is a man both in and out of his scientific time. His retro-styling and youthful hubris lend a satirical edge to the writing. His experiments are of rather dubious parentage, inspired by alchemy, and this sets him at odds with his university teachers at Ingolstadt, Krempe and Waldman. These professors represent a debate about the nature of science, particularly in the developing institutions. Both oppose modern chemistry to alchemy, as a humbler, more incremental and yet more progressive form of science. Krempe eschews the grandiose ambitions and speculations of the alchemists, while Waldman to some extent recuperates them under the rubric of the 'man of genius' (vol. I, ch. II):

> He said, that 'these were men to whose indefatigable zeal modern philosophers were indebted for most of the foundations of their knowledge. They had left to us, as an easier task, to give new names, and arrange in connected classifications, the facts which they in great degree had been the instruments of bringing to light. The labours of men of genius, however erroneously directed, scarcely ever fail in ultimately turning to the solid advantage of mankind.'

In a parody of the Romantic Prometheus as heroic individual, Frankenstein aspires to being the man of genius and, encouraged by his alchemical influences, pursues an extra-curricular vocation to discover the source of life. His experiment, however, rebounds on him. As well as over-reaching, he is also rather incompetent, foolish and unpleasant. The explorer Walton, who is so attracted to Frankenstein, shares many of these characteristics. In the first edition, at least, there is also a hint of incest in Frankenstein's marriage to his cousin and childhood playmate Elizabeth, not to mention something slightly creepy about his father's own marriage (vol. I, ch. I).

Frankenstein is clearly something of a grotesque, but the novel is not a critique of materialism, science and its ambitions, and a reinstatement of the claims of religion. Frankenstein's research draws heavily on the contemporary debate over 'vitalism', which held that there was a soul or animating force 'analogous to electricity', in addition to the matter of the body. Its advocates were seeking to check the dangerous implications of materialism, whose arguments were marshalled at the time particularly by William Lawrence, part of the wider network of Shelley contacts, who located his materialist science with progressive ideas in other fields, including politics and ethics.[38] Clearly, Frankenstein is no radical Lawrentian. The theory he works with is essentially the vitalist third way between science and religion, crossed with the megalomanic and quasi-magical claims of alchemy. There is a sceptical and sardonic attitude towards the claims of professional scientists, but Shelley seems to be poking fun at the particular implications of the vitalist compromise.

More, however, is said about rationality and progress through the creature himself. He is a new Adam, but also has Promethean characteristics and represents the potential of human development. In the novel, compared with its many adaptations, the monster develops into a complex being, in many ways the most attractive figure in the book. The centrepiece of the novel (vol. II) is the confrontation between Frankenstein and the creature, where not only are there competing perspectives on events, but also an extensive account of the interior voice and emerging consciousness of the creature. He recalls how, after initially discovering his motor and sensory functions (vol. II, ch. III), he developed self-awareness and the ability to reflect (vol. II, ch. V):

As I read, however, I applied much personally to my own feelings and condition. I found myself similar, yet at the same time strangely unlike the beings concerning whom I read, and to whose conversation I was a listener. I sympathized with and partly understood them, but I was unformed in mind; I was dependent on none, and related to none. 'The path of my departure was free;' and there was none to lament my annihilation. My person was hideous, and my stature gigantic: what did this mean? Who was I? What was I? Whence did I come? What was my destination? These questions continually recurred, but I was unable to resolve them.

The creature learns speech, develops intellectually and morally, and teaches himself the rudiments of a radical and Romantic education. The creature overhears Volney's *Ruins of Empire*, an account of ancient and modern empires, the role of religion in sustaining them, and of revolutions within them; he acquires *Paradise Lost*, Goethe's Sturm und Drang talisman, *The Sorrows of Young Werther*, and Plutarch's *Lives* (vol. II, ch. VII; p. 103 Butler). In addition to Volney's political sweep, these books provide accounts of grand, if flawed, individuals within strongly ethical narratives. The creature is remorseless and terrifying, yes, but remorseless and terrifyingly moral.

The creature both exemplifies human development and dramatises its limitations. What he craves is society. For a while, he entertains notions of being accepted, but his rejection by the De Laceys leads to the first crisis. Driven away from society, his actions only serve, however accidentally, to alienate him further and demand from his creator a mate. In a rewriting of Milton – the creature explicitly contrasts himself with Satan (vol. II, ch. V) – the creator, Frankenstein, is terrorised into continuing his actions but ultimately refuses to follow through. Frankenstein claims that the creature wants to breed and then to wage war on humanity. This is not certainly true and seems rather to represent the projection of his own fears (or desires) and inability to deal with difference. If the novel is a tragedy, the tragedy belongs to the monster, a tragedy of Promethean isolation and torment.

Abandoned by his creator and self-taught, the monster represents human development. *Frankenstein* stands, then, in the tradition that emancipates humans from a creator – in that sense it is consonant with the Prometheus of Romantic poetry. At the same time, it dramatises through both the monster and Frankenstein himself the need for society, community and, indeed, family. Society is not, however, idealised. Indeed, one of the issues repeatedly picked up in cinematic receptions is the nature of society and difference. The novel raises questions about the position of science without a humanistic orientation, but also asks questions about the nature and implications of humanism itself. Is humanity is any measure of humanism?

This provocative and complex novel is further complicated by the revisions made for the 1831 edition. By this point, there was a backlash against radical science and in some respects the culture became much more closed. The book's early reception, despite some critical nervousness, had already redirected the narrative in moralising terms. The revisions make concessions in this direction, close down some of the questions raised and underplay the satirical edge. Scientific concerns become less specific, and Frankenstein himself becomes distanced from technical science towards metaphysical speculation (Ch. III; p. 213 Butler[39]):

> Chance – or rather the evil influence, the Angel of Destruction, which asserted omnipotent sway over me from the moment I turned my reluctant steps from my father's door – led me first to Mr. Krempe, professor of natural philosophy. He was an uncouth man, but deeply embued in the secrets of his science. He asked me several questions concerning my progress in the different branches of science appertaining to natural philosophy. I replied carelessly; and, partly in contempt, mentioned the names of my alchymists as the principal authors I had studied.

His character becomes nobler and less sleazy. Evil and fate are increasingly flagged as the driving forces in the novel. This underplays Frankenstein's responsibility in favour of more cosmic sources. The revisions do not wholly obscure the issues of the first edition, but orient the novel towards morality tale, rather than an unsettling investigation of both rationalism and humanism.

Frankenstein can be read as a commentary on the Prometheus of the Romantic poets. Both the famous episode of the ghost-stories at which the kernel of *Frankenstein* was presented and the composition of Byron's *Prometheus* occurred in the summer of 1816 at the Villa Diodati. *Frankenstein* itself, published in March 1818, predates the initial composition of *Prometheus Unbound* in the summer of that year, but Promethean ideas were clearly circulating within the group and Shelley had been engaged with Aeschylus and *Prometheus Bound* in particular (and discussing them with Mary) since at least 1814.[40] Although the Romantics radically altered the nature of poetry, criticism and the figure of Prometheus specifically, the vision of *Frankenstein* has proved the most fertile for subsequent reception.

As well as sparking a rich tradition of horror, primarily through the 1931 film directed by James Whale, *Frankenstein* has been claimed as one of the founding works of the genre of science fiction, particularly by the novelist and historian of science fiction, Brian Aldiss.[41] *Frankenstein* lies directly or indirectly behind many of the narratives of the creation and development of artificial life and intelligence.[42] At one remove is Prometheus. The influence of *Prometheus Bound* itself upon science-fiction narratives is thus largely of a second-order kind, but as the godfather of human progress, rationalism and science, he is repeatedly invoked, from Zamyatin's dystopian *We* to Stanislav Lem's *Solaris* and beyond.[43] A recent exception to this generalisation is Hal Duncan's recent novel, *Vellum* (2006), which used the Prometheus myth and its specific incarnation in *Prometheus Bound* as part of multiple-stranded allegory.

After Shelley's *Prometheus Unbound*, large-scale, confrontational and influential literary reworkings are harder to find. Melville's *Moby Dick* is a characteristically enigmatic exception; even more enigmatic is André Gide's absurdist *Prométhée mal enchaîné* (*Prometheus Ill-bound*, 1899).[44] It is possible, however, to see the Promethean theme taken up and reworked more subtly. It is used notably by women responding to and critiquing both the Miltonic heritage and their male contemporaries. Mary Shelley's reading of the myth is only the most explicit such example.[45]

The Aeschylean play continued to be popular throughout the nineteenth century, to judge by the number of translations, although most of these were of the 'crib' variety, reflecting the growing institutional importance of Classics in the nineteenth century.[46] As with the creative adaptations and reworkings, it is again striking that women are to the fore in translating Aeschylus, and *Prometheus Bound* in particular. The most well-known of these are the two versions by Elizabeth Barrett Browning (1833 and 1850).[47] Lorna Hardwick has noted that a number of these translators would go on to play a role in the emerging campaign for women's suffrage and other radical movements, and that translating Aeschylus was a kind of rite of passage for radical women in the period.[48]

The materialist orientation is also reflected within political culture. Indeed, as I noted at the beginning of the book, one of the most significant readers of *Prometheus Bound* was Karl Marx, influenced here as elsewhere by German Romanticism. The attractions of Prometheus are obvious: representative of progress, freedom, economic, industrial and social development. The marrying of a progressive political and social agenda to a scientific agenda is consonant with the orientation of *Frankenstein*. Both Victor and his creature, however, bring anxieties to the Promethean myth: are human nature or human society really up to the expectations of a Percy Shelley or a Marx?

The twentieth-century politics of Prometheus

The Prometheus of the twentieth century was a clear development of the Romantic and Enlightenment Prometheus, an allegory of science and human progress, sometimes as a code for atheism (which can be tracked back through Marx and the emancipatory Romantic Prometheus to the over-reaching allegory of the Renaissance). The association with radical politics continued, both in a Romantic spirit, with the emphasis on freedom and liberation from tyranny, and increasingly as a more specific symbol of socialist struggles in and through the industrial working class. Building on Marx's own enthusiasm, Prometheus became a doubly important Soviet symbol, both for policies of rapid industrialisation and for the claims of Marxism to being a scientific doctrine, which go back to Engels.[49] Creative reworkings and performances of *Prometheus Bound* have exploited its formal peculiarities to make striking cultural and political interventions. Towards the end of the century, however, the political allegiance of Prometheus shifted, reflecting both international politics and the increasing dissociation of science from radical politics. At the beginning of the twenty-first century, Prometheus is encountered as the casual emblem of global capital or of techno-libertarianism as often as he is of political revolution.[50] The element of hope has been conspicuously removed, as works have confronted deindustrialisation and revolutionary failure. Running as a thread through much of this is consideration of the classical past as a tool for liberation or reaction.

Prometheus Bound is not the most frequently staged Aeschylean tragedy, coming well behind the *Oresteia* plays,[51] but there have been notable stagings and adaptations, particularly in Greece itself. One of the more celebrated instances was that which formed the centrepiece of the Delphi festival of 1927, directed by Eva Palmer (revived in 1930). This version was notable for its music, choreography and dance, with a varied set of influences that included Nietzsche's theory of tragedy (for whom, under the influence of Wagner, *Prometheus Bound* and Prometheus were exemplary[52]), the dance of Isadora Duncan, and Greek folk performance. This performance firmly established the practice of putting on Greek drama in the rediscovered classical theatres and also the use of masks in performance. Some parts were filmed by the Gaziadis brothers (1927, revised 1971).[53] *Prometheus Bound* has likewise often proved attractive to directors seeking to find modes of theatrical expression beyond the naturalistic – one director reflecting on productions of the 1960s has linked the 'total theatre' of Aeschylus with a variety of alternative modes, including Brechtian performance and Theatre of the Absurd.[54] Such modes of performance are often strongly political, again best seen in the play's production history in Greece. Firmly established in the Greek repertoire, the politics of *Prometheus Bound* were far from neutral in the political conflicts that convulsed Greece after the Second World War. During the junta of the Colonels (1967-74), classical drama was one site of ideological and cultural struggle. Prometheus and Antigone, the two rebels of Greek tragedy *par excellence*, became central. But opposition was rooted not only in the characters and stories, but the form of Greek tragedy, whose modes of performance and audience provocation were at odds with the kitsch realism more favoured by the regime.[55]

A number of provocative musical adaptations have also related political intervention and formal innovation. Among the more striking aspects of Soviet aesthetics is experimentation in integrated light and music displays, which took their cue from Scriabin's *Prometheus: the Poem of Fire*, but which developed as a specific aesthetic genre.[56] More recent musical adaptations of *Prometheus Bound* offer a contrasting pair. Carl Orff's setting of the Aeschylean Greek (1968) is a striking exercise in defamiliarisation, which emphasises the intensity and grandeur of the play within a broadly conservative frame. In a wholly different vein from Orff's grandiloquent literalism is the complex and experimental piece by Luigi Nono, *Prometeo: Tragedia dell'ascolto* (*Prometheus: Tragedy of Listening*, 1981/1985), which draws on a wide range of influences and texts from Hesiod and Aeschylus to the cultural theorist Walter Benjamin.

A number of English-language poets have offered versions of the play, including Tom Paulin and Robert Lowell.[57] One of the most provocative recent reworkings is Tony Harrison's 1998 film, *Prometheus*, a work with striking imagery, but which lacks coherence. Although set up as a work of ideologically committed film-making – Harrison's own notes refer to, amongst others, Eisenstein – its ideological position is at best confusing.[58] Like Mary Shelley and Marx, Harrison's concern is with technology and progress, scientific and social. But where Shelley's narrative foregrounds a broad investigation of the aims, progress and ethics of science, the nature of humanity and the role of humanism, Harrison's scope is much more circumscribed, aporetic and pessimistic.

The film is oriented around the closure of the last Yorkshire pit and presents a confrontation between the representatives of the old and the new, socialism and capitalism. In the red corner is old grandad, a retired miner proudly dying of smoker's and miner's lung. He is aided by his daydreaming grandson, who is reading about Prometheus at school. In the blue corner is Hermes, representative of Zeus and business, aided by Kratos and Bia, drivers-cum-henchmen. Hermes is a pantomime villain, an effete southerner set against the manly miners. Zeus' spin doctor, he alludes to the architect of New Labour, Peter Mandelson. Issues of sexuality are to the fore, in glaringly unreconstructed form: the silver jumpsuit and eye-shadow are particularly unsubtle.

Grandad's defiance and ultimate martyrdom in a burning cinema encourage the audience to take his side, and there is some suggestion that Zeus is responsible for man's misfortunes, but ironically Hermes, like Milton's Satan, dominates his work. Grandad heroises Prometheus, but Hermes orchestrates the narrative and describes the negative implications of fire and industry – disabled miners, massive environmental damage (Scene 72), industrialised war (Scene 104), industrialised genocide (Scene 121). Smoking, championed by Grandad, is killing him (Scene 72). As Harrison piles on the issues, it is striking how little the Prometheans have to say for themselves. Prometheus is reduced to a golden statue carted across Europe to its final indignities amidst the oil-refineries of Eleusis. The film suggests that the theft of fire has rebounded and that fire, socialism, and progress are an exhausted seam. Progress is equated with heavy industry, as in, e.g., Scene 124, and the film is for the most part an elegy on the decline of industry and the industrial working class.[59] Capital, it appears, has triumphed (Scene 161):

> Hermes.
> Isn't it frightening a few notes
> Can make Prometheans turn their coats?

Again, Grandad in despair:

> He's killing two birds with one stone
> The spirit of Prometheus, and your own.

And if the current situation is terrible, there is very little suggestion of any alternative possibilities.

Hermes oversees the destruction of the mining community, which consists of uniformly traditional nuclear families. The husbands, miners, are trapped in a van and driven to Europe, where they are melted down for the statue of Prometheus. The wives, who work in the fish-factory of Okeanos, are encased in the plastic sheeting that delimits their work space and meta- morphosed into a chorus of mutely wailing tailor's dummies, who are floated down the Humber and over the sea to Prometheus' final resting-place. But the key figure in the deg- radation of the community is the boy's mam, in the Io role. She is driven by Hermes' henchmen over Europe, in a Grand Tour of humanity's inhumanity, before she is killed in a slaughter- house. In *Prometheus Bound*, Io and the chorus have a voice, express their thoughts and feelings and come to far less horrific fates. As I argued in Chapter 2, they are proxies for humanity in general, their suffering, solidarity and hope. Harrison denies them this and instead dramatises a crisis of masculinity. The women in the community are threatening to become the domi- nant breadwinners. It is hard not to see in their enveloping and their silencing, a punishment for daring to work at all. Harri- son's *Prometheus* is reactionary as well as nostalgically elegiac. Questions of diversity, tolerance or sympathy that are central to the account of progress in *Prometheus Bound* and its reception are ignored. The idea of progress itself is under threat: the alternatives seem to be either unbridled capitalism or unbridled self-harm, neither a social good.

As in so much Promethean reception, the film is self-conscious, but again there is uncertainty. Harrison (Scenes 63 and 104) inherits the Romantic, heroising view of poetry that Shelley explores in his introduction to *Prometheus Unbound*, but just as with the myth of progress, the liberating force of poetry, of education, is restricted. Poetry is a mark of gods, not mortals – Hermes speaks in verse; Grandad and especially the doomed miners appear to have it imposed on them. Hermes equates fire with poetry (Scene 114) and worries about Olympus falling 'if *poetry* should come to *Pontefract*' (Scene 63), but there seems to be little danger of either. Hermes sneers at the ignorant audience, recounting the Aeschylean life and quoting ancient Greek, neither of which they are expected to know or understand. The boy (wholly implausibly) is being made to learn chunks of Aeschylus by rote, the value of which is met with acute scepticism by his father (Scene 20). Ultimately, Hermes circumscribes the ideological scope of poetry (Scene 162).

> And poor mortals think that song redeems
> The ravages of such regimes.

Hermes' cynicism is undoubtedly realistic, but both the presentation of fire-as-poetry and fire-as-heavy-industry illustrate nothing so much as a crisis in the traditional Left. In Harrison's *Prometheus*, there seems no role for Promethean hope, no role for the idea of progress, material or cultural.

Reclaiming progress

Prometheus Bound has had a vibrant history of reception, not least in English and German radical circles. A series of interventions in different media have used the play to think through the nature of human cultural, technological and political progress, to explore the nature of political intervention and political activism, and to reflect upon the relationship of culture and politics. These interventions also afford the opportunity to reflect upon different facets of the Aeschylean play. At the same time, *Prometheus Bound* and its reception invite consideration of the place of Classics, inside and outside any institutional frame. To what extent can Classics be integrated into a progressive, liberatory education, rather than being co-opted as a means of reifying the past and shoring up traditional power structures?

The changing cultural and political environment has clearly shaped those responses and at the beginning of the twenty-first century, there is a crisis for the narrative of political and scientific/industrial progress that has developed since the Romantics and shaped particularly by socialism. As the Right have increasingly co-opted Prometheanism, shorn of its political bite, for a neutral technocratic progress or indeed a celebration of capital, the optimistic narrative on the Left has retreated. Arguments about technology, politics and progress continue, however, in this more contested space and there is ample scope for the reclamation of a fully Promethean voice. I await future developments with interest.

Abbreviations and Guide to Further Reading

Abbreviations

ABV = J.D. Beazley, *Attic Black-Figure Vase-Painters* (Oxford: Clarendon Press, 1956).

Ath. Pol. = [Aristotle], *The Athenian Constitution* (*Athenaiôn Politeia*). Text: F.G. Kenyon (Oxford: Clarendon Press, 1920); M. Chambers (Leipzig: Teubner, 1986). Translations, with helpful notes, by P.J. Rhodes (Harmondsworth: Penguin, 1984) or J.M. Moore, in *Aristotle and Xenophon on Democracy and Oligarchy* (Berkeley/London: University of California Press, 1986). Full commentary by Rhodes (Oxford: Clarendon Press, 1992).

D-K = H. Diels and W. Kranz (eds), *Die Fragmente der Vorsokratiker*, 7th edn (Berlin: Weidmann, 1954).

FGH = F. Jacoby (ed.), *Die Fragmente der griechischen Historiker* (Berlin: Weidmann/Leiden: Brill, 1923-).

IG = *Inscriptiones Graecae* (Berlin, 1873-).

ML = R. Meiggs and D.M. Lewis (eds), *A Selection of Greek Historical Inscriptions to the End of the Fifth century BC*, rev. edn (Oxford: Clarendon Press, 1988).

PMG = D.L. Page (ed.), *Poetae Melici Graeci* (Oxford: Clarendon Press, 1962).

Aeschylus: texts and translations

D.L. Page (ed.), *Aeschyli septem quae supersunt tragoedias* (Oxford: Clarendon Press, 1972).

A.H. Sommerstein (ed.), *Aeschylus* (Cambridge, Mass.: Harvard University Press, 2009). Text and translation; includes a volume of fragments, including *Prometheus Unbound.*

B. Snell, S.L. Radt and R. Kannicht (eds), *Tragicorum graecorum fragmenta* (Göttingen: Vandenhoeck & Ruprecht, 1971-2004). The standard edition of fragments.

M.L. West (ed.), *Aeschyli tragoediae, cum incerti poetae Prometheo* (Stuttgart: Teubner, 1990).

Prometheus Bound: editions and commentaries

M. Griffith (ed.), *Aeschylus: Prometheus Bound* (Cambridge: Cambridge University Press, 1983). Text and indispensable commentary, even for those without Greek.
A.J. Podlecki (ed.), *Aeschylus: Prometheus Bound* (Warminster: Aris and Phillips, 2005). Text, translation and commentary, keyed to the translation.
G. Thomson (ed.), *The Prometheus Bound* (Cambridge: Cambridge University Press, 1932). Dated, but still useful.

Prometheus Bound: English translations

C. Collard (tr.), *Aeschylus: Persians and Other Plays* (Oxford: Oxford University Press, 2009). The most modern translation, with excellent introduction and notes.
D. Grene, in D. Grene and R. Lattimore (trs), *Aeschylus* (Chicago: University of Chicago Press, 1956). Still, for many, the classic series of translations of Greek tragedy.
C.J. Herington and J. Scully (trs), *Aeschylus: Prometheus Bound* (New Haven/London: Yale University Press, 1975).
P. Vellacott (tr.), *Aeschylus: Prometheus Bound and Other Plays* (Harmondsworth: Penguin, 1961). Beginning to show its age.
See also Thomson and Sommerstein (above).

General works on Greek tragedy

E. Csapo and W.J. Slater, *The Context of Ancient Drama* (Ann Arbor: University of Michigan Press, 1995). Source book for the production and festival context of Greek drama, with texts in translation.
P.E. Easterling (ed.), *The Cambridge Companion to Greek Tragedy* (Cambridge: Cambridge University Press, 1997). Essays on many aspects, from a mainly historicist approach.
S. Goldhill, *Reading Greek Tragedy* (Cambridge: Cambridge University Press, 1986). Discusses Greek tragedy using modern critical approaches.
J. Gregory (ed.), *A Companion to Greek Tragedy* (Oxford: Blackwell, 2005). More comprehensive than the *Cambridge Companion*.
A.W. Pickard-Cambridge, *The Dramatic Festivals of Athens*, 2nd edn (Oxford: Clarendon Press, 1988). The standard discussion and compendium on the production and context of Greek drama; sources are in Greek.

O.P. Taplin, *Greek Tragedy in Action* (London: Methuen, 1978). Approaches Greek drama from the point of view of theatrical production.

Aeschylus: general works

M. Gagarin, *Aeschylean Drama* (University of California Press: Berkeley, 1976).

A.J. Podlecki, *The Political Background of Aeschylean Tragedy*, 2nd edn (London: Bristol Classical Press, 1999).

T.G. Rosenmeyer, *The Art of Aeschylus* (University of California Press: Berkeley/London, 1982).

K. Reinhardt, *Aischylos als Regisseur und Theologe* (Bern: Francke, 1949).

F. Solmsen, *Hesiod and Aeschylus* (Ithaca/London: Cornell University Press, 1949).

A.H. Sommerstein, *Aeschylean Tragedy*, 2nd edn (Duckworth: London, 2010). This differs in important respects from the first edition.

O.P. Taplin, *The Stagecraft of Aeschylus* (Oxford: Clarendon Press, 1977). Detailed analysis of Aeschylus in the ancient theatre.

G. Thomson, *Aeschylus and Athens: A Study in the Social Origins of Drama*, 4th edn (London: Lawrence & Wishart, 1973). A provocative sociological approach from a non-orthodox Marxist perspective.

R.P. Winnington-Ingram, *Studies in Aeschylus* (Cambridge: Cambridge University Press, 1983).

Historical context

J.K. Davies, *Democracy and Classical Greece*, 2nd edn (London: Fontana, 1993).

C.W. Fornara (ed.), *Archaic Times To The End Of The Peloponnesian War*, volume 1 (Cambridge: Cambridge University Press, 1983). Sources in translation: inscriptions from ML, plus other material.

W.G.G. Forrest, *The Emergence of Greek Democracy: the Character of Greek Politics, 800-400 B.C.* (London: Weidenfeld & Nicolson, 1966).

S. Hornblower, *The Greek World, 479-323 BC*, 3rd edn (London: Routledge, 2002)

P. Low (ed.), *The Athenian Empire* (Edinburgh: Edinburgh University Press, 2008). Collects important articles on the Athenian empire.

R. Meiggs, *The Athenian Empire* (Oxford: Oxford University Press, 1972)

R.G. Osborne, S. Hornblower and M. C. Greenstock (eds.), *The Athenian Empire*, LACTOR, 4th edn (Harrow: London Association of Classical Teachers, 1983). Sources in translation.

P.J. Rhodes, *A History of the Classical Greek World 478-323 BC* (Malden, Mass./Oxford: Blackwell, 2006).

General studies of *Prometheus Bound*

D.J. Conacher, *Aeschylus' Prometheus Bound. A Literary Commentary* (Toronto: University of Toronto Press, 1980).

L. Golden, *In Praise of Prometheus: Humanism and Rationalism in Aeschylean Thought* (Chapel Hill: University of North Carolina Press, 1966).

M. Griffith, 'Aeschylus, Sicily and Prometheus', in: R.D. Dawe, J. Diggle and P.E. Easterling (eds), *Dionysiaca: Nine Studies in Greek Poetry by Former Pupils, Presented to Denys Page on his Seventieth Birthday* (Cambridge: Cambridge Faculty Library, 1978), 105-39.

H. Lloyd-Jones, 'Zeus, Prometheus, and Greek Ethics', *Harvard Studies in Classical Philology* 101 (2003), 49-72. With references to earlier discussions.

T.G. Rosenmeyer, '*Prometheus Bound*: Tragedy or Treatise?', in *The Masks of Tragedy: Essays on Six Greek Dramas* (New York: Gordian Press, 1971), 49-102.

R. Unterberger, *Der gefesselte Prometheus des Aischylos. Eine Interpretation* (Stuttgart: Kohlhammer, 1968).

M.L. West, 'The Prometheus Trilogy', *Journal of Hellenic Studies* 99 (1979), 130-48.

See also chapters in Podlecki, Solmsen, Sommerstein, Thomson, Winnington-Ingram, above.

Date and authenticity

R. Bees, *Zur Datierung des Prometheus Desmotes* (Stuttgart: Teubner, 1993).

E.R. Dodds, 'The *Prometheus Vinctus* and the Progress of Scholarship', in *The Ancient Concept of Progress, and Other Essays on Greek Literature and Belief* (Oxford: Clarendon Press, 1973), 26-44.

M. Griffith, *The Authenticity of Prometheus Bound* (Cambridge: Cambridge University Press, 1977). The standard account, with earlier bibliography.

C.J. Herington, *The Author of the Prometheus Bound* (Austin, Tx.: University of Texas Press, 1970). Not as full (or as sceptical) as Griffith.

P. Pattoni, *L'autenticità del Prometeo incatenato di Eschilo* (Pisa: Scuola Normale Superiore, 1987). A critique of Griffith.

M.L. West, *Studies in Aeschylus* (Stuttgart: Teubner, 1990). Includes a polemical attack on *Prometheus Bound*.

See also Taplin, *Stagecraft* above (another polemical attack).

Poetic and philosophical context

J. Barnes (tr.), *Early Greek Philosophy*, new edn (London: Penguin, 2002). Presocratic philosophers in translation.

M. Gagarin and P. Woodruff (trs), *Early Greek Political Thought from Homer to the Sophists* (Cambridge: Cambridge University Press, 1995). Includes important material from the sophists.

W.K.C. Guthrie, *A History of Greek Philosophy* (Cambridge: Cambridge University Press, 1962-81). Vols I-II have presocratic material; III includes the sophists (also published separately)

E. Hussey, *The Presocratics*, new edn (London: Bristol Classical Press, 1998). Helpful introductory account of presocratic philosophy.

G.B. Kerferd, *The Sophistic Movement* (Cambridge: Cambridge University Press, 1981). A key discussion of the sophists.

C.C.W. Taylor (tr.), *Plato: Protagoras*, rev. edn (Oxford: Clarendon Press, 1991). English text and full commentary.

R. Waterfield (tr.), *The First Philosophers: the Presocratics and Sophists* (Oxford: Oxford University Press, 2000). Translations, notes and useful bibliographies.

M.L. West (tr.), *Hesiod: Theogony and Works and Days* (Oxford: Oxford University Press, 1998). Translation with very useful notes (for more detail, see his commentaries on the poems).

Staging

J. Davidson, '*Prometheus Vinctus* on the Athenian Stage', *Greece and Rome* 41.1 (1994), 33-40.

E. Fraenkel, 'Der Einzug des Chors im *Prometheus*', *Annali della Scuola Normale Superiore di Pisa, Cl. di Lettere e Filosofia* 23 (1954), 269-84, reprinted in *Kleine Beiträge zur klassischen Philologie* (Rome: Edizioni di storia e letteratura), I.389-406.

G. Thomson, 'Notes on *Prometheus Vinctus*', *Classical Quarterly* 23.3/4 (1929), 155-63.

See also Griffith, *Authenticity* and *Prometheus Bound*, Taplin, *Stagecraft*, Sommerstein, *Aeschylean Tragedy*, West, 'The Prometheus Trilogy'.

Language and imagery

B.H. Fowler, 'The Imagery of the *Prometheus Bound*', *American Journal of Philology* 78.2 (1957), 173-84.

H.S. Long, 'Notes on Aeschylus' *Prometheus Bound*', *Proceedings of the American Philosophical Society* 102 (1958), 229-80.

J.M. Mossman, 'Chains of Imagery in *Prometheus Bound*', *Classical Quarterly* 46.1 (1996), 58-67.

E. Petrounias, *Funktion und Thematik der Bilder bei Aischylos* (Göttingen: Vandenhoeck & Ruprecht, 1978). Standard account of Aeschylean imagery, including a chapter on *Prometheus Bound*.

Reception

C. Dougherty, *Prometheus* (London: Routledge, 2005).

J. Duchemin, *Prométhée: histoire du mythe, de ses origines orientales à ses incarnations modernes* (Paris: Les Belles Lettres, 1974).

J.A. Gruys, *The Early Printed Editions (1518-1664) of Aeschylus: a Chapter in the History of Classical Scholarship*, *Bibliotheca humanistica & reformatorica* 32 (Nieuwkoop: de Graaf, 1981).

L. Hardwick (ed.), *Tony Harrison's Poetry, Drama and Film: The Classical Dimension*, *Open Colloquium* (Milton Keynes: The Open University, October 1999).

K. Kerenyi, *Prometheus: Archetypal Image of Human Existence* (London: Thames & Hudson, 1963).

C. Kreutz, *Das Prometheussymbol in der Dichtung der englischen Romantik*, *Palaestra* 236 (Göttingen: Vandenhoeck & Ruprecht, 1963).

L.M. Lewis, *The Promethean Politics of Milton, Blake and Shelley* (Columbia/London: University of Missouri Press, 1992).

M. Mund-Dopchie, *La survie d'Eschyle à la Renaissance* (Louvain: Peeters, 1984).

F. Macintosh, 'The "Rediscovery" of Aeschylus for the Modern Stage', in: J. Jouanna and F. Montanari (eds), *Éschyle à l'aube du théâtre occidental: neuf exposés suivis de discussions* (Geneva: Fondation Hardt, 2008), 435-68.

R. Trousson, *Le Thème de Prométhée dans la littérature européenne*, 2 vols (Geneva: Librairie Droz, 1964).

See also West, *Studies* for the history of the text.

Notes

1. Themes, Contexts and Receptions

1. In an unpublished foreword (1841) to his doctoral dissertation: Marx and Engels, *MECW*, I.31.

2. Political: Taplin, *Stagecraft*, 469; irreligious: M.L. West, *Studies*, 53.

3. Weiss, *Marat/Sade* (see also the English translation).

4. For the division of Greek tragedy into structural parts, see Aristotle, *Poetics* 1452b14-17. There is debate as to whether these are either Aristotelian or useful: see Taplin, *Stagecraft*, 470-6; more positively evaluated by Mastronarde, *Euripides: Medea*, 74-80, with bibliography, and elaborated in the formal approaches in Jens.

5. For dates, see Suda αι57 and π2230, Parian Marble A59 and A48; on the ancient life, see Lefkowitz.

6. For *Prometheus Pyrkaeus*, see Pollux, *Onomastikon* 9.156, 10.64; cf. Garvie, *Persians*, xlv. On connected Aeschylean tetralogies, see Gantz.

7. See Garvie, *Suppliants*, 1-28. For Sophokles' first performance and victory, see Plutarch, *Kimon* 8.7-9.

8. Griffith, *Authenticity*, 226-45, who slightly underplays the readiness of ancient scholars to dispute authorship.

9. See Flintoff, 'Aristophanes and the *Prometheus Bound*', 2-4.

10. Doubts over *Prometheus Bound* start with Westphal. For the end of *Seven*, see Hutchinson, 209-11, with bibliography.

11. Especially Schmid; see Lloyd-Jones, 'Zeus in Aeschylus', 55-6, Dodds, 'Progress', 30-6.

12. M.L. West, *Studies*, 53; Taplin, *Stagecraft*, 466-9.

13. The most extensive study is by Petrounias, 97-126, who sees *Prometheus Bound* as compatible with Aeschylus generally; for the alternative view, see Griffith, *Prometheus Bound*, 20.

14. 'Recitative' (*parakatalogê*) seems to have been faster than speech and reflected a heightening of emotion: see [Aristotle], *Problems* 918a10-12 and generally Pickard-Cambridge, 157-67.

15. Pattoni's is the most systematic attempt to question the statistics, but it does not overturn the entire edifice.

16. The lack of comparative material is stressed, e.g., by Zuntz.

17. See, e.g., Griffith, *Authenticity*, 84 and 101-2.

18. Hubbard argues that variation in anapaests is in actors' recitative and driven by context, and can be paralleled in other Aeschylean plays.

19. For the late development, see especially Herington, *Author*. For Sicily, see especially Focke, with criticism from Griffith, 'Sicily'.

20. Aristias, second to Aeschylus' Oedipus trilogy in 467 with plays by his father, Pratinas; Iophon, son of Sophokles; and Araros, son of Aristophanes. See Griffith, *Authenticity*, 226-7, 254, who discusses several possible poets writing in the Aeschylean tradition. Euphorion or another relative was suggested by Robertson, 'On the Chronology of Aeschylus'. Euphorion was further championed by Dodds, 'Progress', 37-40 and adopted by M.L. West, *Studies*, 67-72 and Sommerstein, *Aeschylean Tragedy*, 232.

21. *Prometheus Unbound* is also the next play alphabetically and Griffith, *Authenticity*, 13 suggests that it refers to an alphabetic edition of plays, although there is no good parallel for such a comment in dramatic scholia (cf. M.L. West, 'The Prometheus Trilogy', 130 n. 2); Griffith compares Σ Pindar, *Isthmian* 3.24, which is not decisive.

22. cf. Griffith, *Prometheus Bound*, 284.

23. A.L. Brown; Sommerstein, *Aeschylean Tragedy*, 227-8.

24. Lloyd-Jones, *Justice*, 95-103 suggested *Women of Aitna*, written for the foundation of Hieron's city of Aitna; see, however, Taplin, *Stagecraft*, 463-5.

25. Despite Sommerstein, *Aeschylean Tragedy*, 37-9 and 227-8, who argues for a dilogy within a (semi-connected) tetralogy or, more plausibly, as a post-Aeschylean pair for the Lenaia festival where only two tragic plays were put on per poet (competition instituted c.440). For a dilogy, see also the Sicilian hypothesis of Focke, 263-70.

26. *Knights* 758-9 ~ *Prometheus Bound* 59 and *Knights* 836 ~ *Prometheus Bound* 613; for discussions, see Griffith, *Authenticity*, 11 n. 19. M.L. West, 'The Prometheus Trilogy', 132 n. 11 also suggests *Akharnians* 704 ~ *Prometheus Bound* 2, which is not impossible.

27. See Aristophanes, *Akharnians* 9-12. Hutchinson, xlii-xliii is sceptical.

28. The eruption of Aitna occurred in 479 (Parian Marble) or c.475 (Thucydides 3.116); Flintoff, 'The Date of the *Prometheus Bound*', 90-1, in order to secure an early date for the play, is sceptical that a reference to Aitna requires a recent eruption.

29. Both M.L. West, 'The Prometheus Trilogy', 146-7 and Bees adduce further parallels in favour of a late date. For Io, *Suppliant Women* and *Prometheus Bound*, see Murray and Garvie, *Suppliants*, 70-1, 159-60.

30. On actors, see Csapo and Slater, 221, 225-6, and Pickard-Cambridge, 130-2.

31. On formal grounds, earlier scholarship regarded *Prometheus Bound* as 'archaic': see Focke with references.

32. The key, but problematic, literary sources are Thucydides 1.89-113 (the so-called 'Pentecontaetia' covering 479-440) and 1.24-65 (the events of the mid-430s leading to the Peloponnesian War); [Aristotle], *Ath. Pol.* 20-8; Plutarch's *Lives*, especially *Themistokles, Kimon* and *Perikles*; and Diodorus Siculus 11.39-12.28. For useful collections of documentary evidence, see Fornara, *Archaic Times*; Osborne et al.

33. See *Ath. Pol.* 22.2. Herodotos' account of the Athenian command structure at Marathon (6.103-14) is, like much else in that battle, greatly disputed. See also next note.

34. For the introduction of random selection from a group of pre-elected men, see *Ath. Pol.* 22.5; for the procedure, its institution and the consequences, see Rhodes ad loc., with references to alternative views. Rihll, 90-1, is sceptical that the introduction of a random element had any serious impact on the standing of the Areopagus.

35. On ostracism, see [Aristotle], *Ath. Pol.* 22.3-8, with Rhodes ad loc.

36. For Kimon's son, Lakedaimonios, see Thucydides I.45.2, with Hornblower ad loc.

37. For Themistokles' activities after the Persian Wars, see Forrest, 'Themistocles and Argos' (in places speculative). For Ephialtes and Themistokles, see Lewis.

38. Plutarch, *Kimon* 14.3-15.2 (allegedly by Perikles); [Aristotle], *Ath. Pol.* 27.1. For the problematic chronology, see Gomme et al., 389-413 and Hornblower on Thucydides 1.100.2-101 and 1.101.2, with bibliography.

39. Scrutiny: *dokimasia*, before entering office, is favoured by Rihll, *euthynai* on leaving office by Sealey, 'Ephialtes' and 'Ephialtes, *Eisangelia*, and the Council'. The larger case, including *eisangelia* is argued by Rhodes, *The Athenian Boule*, 144-207.

40. The earliest source is Antiphon 5.68, indicating a body but unknown murderers. *Ath. Pol.* 25.4 fingers Aristodikos of Tanagra, which is probably a later invention, as is the claim (Plutarch *Perikles* 10.7-8) that Perikles was behind it: see Roller.

41. Particularly around the battle of Tanagra: Thuc. 1.107.4-6; Plutarch, *Kimon* 17.3-5.

42. Discussions of the politics of the *Oresteia* range beween radical democracy (Dover) and moderation and conservatism (Dodds, 'Progress'). The *Oresteia* is only moderate in the sense that it explains that the centre of Athenian politics has fundamentally shifted and presents a call for unity behind the new order.

43. Especially as the consequences of giving asylum prove extremely grave. For some political explorations, see Winnington-Ingram, 'The Danaid Trilogy of Aeschylus', especially 148-9; Sommerstein,

Aeschylean Tragedy, 100-7; more neutrally, Garvie, *Suppliants*, 197-233.

44. For Perikles as the prosecutor of Kimon at his *euthynai*, see *Ath. Pol.* 27.1.

45. See Meiggs, 'The Crisis of Athenian Imperialism'; Robinson with bibliography. The traditional date of the expedition has been put earlier by Kahn to 462/1-458/7, re-evaluating Diodorus on the basis of the Egyptian evidence.

46. For discussion, see Rhodes, *History*, 71-8.

47. For Sicilian performance, see Lloyd-Jones, 'Zeus, Prometheus, and Greek Ethics', 68-70, with references to earlier attempts in the same direction, especially Focke; see also Griffith, 'Sicily'. For the 'internationalisation' of tragedy, see especially Taplin, 'Spreading the Word'.

2. Gods and Other Monsters

1. For punishment at Athens, see Bonner and Smith, II.279-87, cf. Allen, Griffith on 26.

2. I first wrote this paragraph before defences of torture as investigative practice started becoming a disturbingly familiar part of civic discourse on both sides of the Atlantic.

3. Discussed by Prometheus at 229-31; later he suggests that he himself played a role. For a similar dispute over the source of the Olympians' privileges, see Euripides, *Alkestis* 55. Compare Agamemnon distributing privileges at *Iliad* 9.334, 9.367; for popular consent or distribution, see *Iliad* 1.123, 1.135, 1.276, 16.56, *Odyssey* 7.150; for dispute over the source of privilege, see 1.161-2. Hephaistos uses the term 'honours' (*timas*, 30), which is also highly loaded.

4. See especially Raaflaub, 203-49.

5. Used of Kreon in *Antigone* 60 (associated with powers, *kratê*; but transgression of his authority is associated with violence); associated with profiteering at 1056 and 1169. The use in *Ajax* of Agamemnon (1350) suggests profiteering and is in a highly charged political context (749 is more neutral).

6. *Libation Bearers* 972, with *Agamemnon* 1355, 1365, 1633; cf. *Agamemnon* 828 (of Priam).

7. For the new or young ruler, compare Sophokles, *Antigone* 159-60, 735.

8. Used by Aeschylus of the leaders of Persian troops in various contexts: *Persians* 23, 324, 480 (the latter two in a naval context); cf. also *tagan* used of the Atreidai (*Agamemnon* 110). The term is preferred by Kreon (*Antigone* 1058) in response to reflections on tyranny by Teiresias.

9. *Seven* 2-3, 62, 652. See also *Persians* 767; Sophokles, *Antigone* 994, *Oedipus Tyrannus* 923; Euripides, *Medea* 523.

10. A rare word preserved by Hesychius as a synonym for *athesmôs*, which is unmetrical here. See Griffith, ad loc.

11. A theme in Thucydides, most powerfully at Corcyra (especially 3.82-3).

12. See L.B. Carter. For *hêsykhia* in *Pythian* 8, see Pfeiffer, 426-56 and on 1-2. The ode also uses Typhos, this time as an example of over-riding ambition.

13. For Atlas, see *Theogony* 517-20, with West on 517; Griffith on *Prometheus Bound* 347-50. The picture of Atlas bearing the pillar supporting heaven and earth is a mix of different versions.

14. For 'learning through suffering', *pathei mathos*, see *Agamemnon* 176; it is also evoked by Kratos at 10-11.

15. There are serious textual problems in the third pair of stanzas, which cannot easily be made to correspond metrically. The first of those stanzas may be interpolated: see Griffith ad loc.

16. The ghost may be the gadfly, depending on punctuation: see Griffith on 567.

17. Hermann's supplement of Hera in 600 is accepted by Griffith.

18. Harnessing: 578, 682, 931 (Io); 672 (Inakhos); 5, 54, 71, 108, 176, 323, 562, 618, 1009-10 (Prometheus). Hunt imagery: 571-3 (Io); 856-9 (Io's descendants, the Danaids); 1072, 1078-9 (the chorus of Okeanids); Prometheus refuses to cower like a hunted animal (29, 174, 960). Storm imagery: 643, 746, 838, 885-6 (Io); 563, 1015-16 (Prometheus). For imagery in *Prometheus Bound*, see Fowler, Mossman, Petrounias, 97-126, Griffith, *Prometheus Bound*, 19-21.

19. Earlier stichomythia in the play is much more regular: see Griffith, 29 and Griffith, *Authenticity*, 140-1, with references.

20. For timidity and passivity, see Griffith, *Prometheus Bound*, 22-3; weak, 'irrelevant', un-Aeschylean: Griffith, *Authenticity*, 128-9, 133; but for richer analysis, see Griffith, *Prometheus Bound*, 10-11. For the chorus as a character, see especially Scott, cf. Ewans. In their reactive and timid nature, analogies can be found in the chorus of *Seven*, in particular.

21. *Life of Aeschylus* 88-93 Page = test. 129 Radt.

22. In most cases, the *mêkhanê* was probably not involved in the fifth century. For discussion, see Mastronarde, 'Actors on High'.

23. The other notable abstract entities on the tragic stage are Death (Thanatos) in *Alkestis* (438 BCE) and Madness (Lyssa) in Euripides' *Herakles*.

24. Note also stylistic distance, what Griffith, *Authenticity*, 141 describes as 'archaic formalism'.

25. Lloyd-Jones, 'Zeus in Aeschylus'; see also Lloyd-Jones, *Justice*.

26. A more nuanced position is Lloyd-Jones, 'Zeus, Prometheus, and Greek Ethics', which admits of an element of progression, cf. Lloyd-Jones, *Justice*, 96 n. 101, and follows Unterberger, 138 in allowing that

Zeus changes his political stance. Winnington-Ingram, *Studies*, 180-1 implies that the distinction between a change of political stance and a change of character is over-fine. Denial of progression is maintained by Conacher, *Aeschylus' Prometheus Bound*, 120-37.

27. See also Sommerstein, *Aeschylean Tragedy*, 277-9.

28. Solmsen, 124-6; cf. Sommerstein, *Aeschylean Tragedy*, 277 n. 17.

29. For Zeus and supplication, see 1-4, 26-9, 347, 359-65, 381-6, 625-709 *passim*, 810-6, 1043-73. For discussion, see Lloyd-Jones, 'Zeus in Aeschylus', 57-9.

30. For patriarchy, see especially Zeitlin.

31. Nineteenth-century scholarship often tried to recuperate Zeus or question the value of Promethean progress (see also J.A.K. Thomson, 32-7, Vandvik). For criticism, see Lloyd-Jones, 'Zeus in Aeschylus', 56 and Dodds, 'Progress', 31-5. The scale of the challenge to Zeus is rightly emphasised by Farnell, 45-9.

32. The only (probably) earlier surviving text on the release of the Titans is Pindar, *Pythian* 4.291 (462 BCE).

33. The catalectic anapaestic dimeter at the end of fr. 192 would indicate a change of speaker in *Prometheus Bound* (Griffith, *Prometheus Bound*, 24, 290). The parody in Kratinos' *Wealth Gods* is an exchange between the chorus and another.

34. Here it is explicitly the river Phasis, as in Herodotos 4.45, whereas others such as Hekataios (fr. 195) identify the boundary as the river Tanais (Don), as does Σ Dionysius Periegetes 10 in referring to *Prometheus Unbound* (= fr. VIIc Griffith). In *Prometheus Bound* 734-5 and 790, the Tanais seems indicated: see Chapter 3.

35. See fr. XI, with Griffith ad loc.

36. This is in direct speech, but it is more likely that this was reported in a messenger speech than that the *mêkhanê* was used for the eagle.

37. Σ *Prometheus Bound* 167 = fr. XVc G, which (like Cicero) locates this in the Caucasus, presumably reflecting the common error noted by the *Life of Aeschylus*.

38. Taplin, *Stagecraft*, 431-2 doubts that Zeus appeared in tragedy, even in Aeschylus' *Psykhostasia*.

39. An alternative sequence is provided by Hyginus, *Fabulae* 54 that Herakles' actions were instigated by Zeus in response to Prometheus' warning about Thetis, but this seems at odds with frr. X, XVa and XVc G, as Griffith, *Prometheus Bound*, 301 argues.

40. Victory: Hyginus, *Astronomica* 2.15 = fr. XVI G; punishment: Athenaeus 15.672-3.

41. White argues that there are hints of this too in Io's travels: the places that she will pass through or has passed through on her travels lack *dikê*, which he argues will be supplied by Zeus. In *Prometheus Bound*, however, Zeus himself seems stronger on *adikia*.

42. For Kheiron, see Robertson, 'Prometheus and Chiron', cf. Sommerstein, *Aeschylean Tragedy*, 226 n. 13; for the Promethia, see, for example, G. Thomson, 315; Herington, 'Aeschylus: The Last Phase', 396; for torch races at the Promethia, see Dübner, 211-12, Davies, 'Demosthenes on Liturgies: a Note', 36, and Parke, 171-2. Herington, *Author*, 125, rightly stresses the ingenuity of Aeschylus in the *Eumenides*.

43. On anachronism in Greek tragedy, see Easterling; on 'zooming' effects, see Sourvinou-Inwood, 23-47.

44. See especially Knox, 45-50.

45. See further Chapter 4.

46. Here I follow Gould more than Goldhill, 'Collectivity and Otherness'; for the chorus of Greek tragedy, see also Silk; Mastronarde, 'Knowledge and Authority'; Foley.

47. For the early development of this anti-tyrant stance, see Lavelle, with further bibliography.

48. See the regulations for Erythrai (ML 40.33; *IG* I^3 14.33; Fornara 71A), datable before the mid-440s on letter-forms; possibly 453/2.

49. See Herodotos 5.55-6, 6.109, 123; Thucydides 1.20, 6.53-9; for drinking songs, see Athenaeus 15.695a-b; for celebration at the Panathenaia festival, see Philostratos, *Life of Apollonius of Tyana* 7.4; for offerings (*enagismata*), see [Aristotle], *Ath. Pol.* 58.1; for libations, Demosthenes 19.280; for the inscription on the statues' base, *IG* I^3 502. For discussion of fifth-century reception of the tyrannicides, see M.W. Taylor. R.C.T. Parker, *Athenian Religion*, 136 points out that they are never formally labelled as *hêrôes*.

50. For Themistokles' exile, implication by the Spartans and his escape, see Thucydides 1.135-8; Plutarch, *Themistokles* 22-7. For a (somewhat speculative) account of his activities in the period see Forrest, 'Themistocles and Argos'. For political interpretations of *Prometheus Bound*, see Podlecki, 101-22, who rejects personal allegory, but associates tyrannicide propaganda with Themistokles. Stoessl, 'Aeschylus as a Political Thinker', 129-30 links *Prometheus Bound* to Kimon and Themistokles, predicated on a date in the 470s.

51. For the comic representations and descriptions of Perikles, see Revermann, 'Cratinus' *Dionysalexandros* and the head of Perikles', and Ruffell, 'A Total Write-Off'; a connection between Zeus and Perikles has been argued by Davison, 'The Date of the *Prometheia*', cf. Davison, 'Aeschylus and Athenian Politics', although he argues for a much tighter historical allegory, including Prometheus as code for Protagoras, which I do not accept.

52. Thucydides 2.65.3-4; Plutarch, *Perikles* 35.4; Diodorus Siculus 12.45.4. This allusion to *dêmokratia* is slightly more direct than, but reminiscent of, the earliest allusion to the concept at Aeschylus, *Suppliant Women* 604.

143

53. For discussion, see Ruffell, 'The World Turned Upside Down', 475-81 and Bakola, 122-41; cf. M.L. West, 'The Prometheus Trilogy', 141, Griffith, *Prometheus Bound*, 288.

54. Ruffell, 'A Total Write-Off' argues that the allegorical technique of *Knights* is similar to a number of plays by Kratinos in this respect.

3. Technology and Civilisation

1. For an emphasis on universals over the immediate political context, see the powerful statement of Macleod. Much debate in the past two decades has focused on the implications of the institutional context, in response to Goldhill, 'Great Dionysia', and is summarised by D.M. Carter, *Politics of Greek Tragedy*, especially 35-55. Rhodes, 'Nothing', for example, accepts the civic context but rejects any democratic particularity. For consideration of the form of tragedy as democratic, see Burian. My arguments do not depend on either the institutional context or the form of tragedy.

2. Jones, 41-72, especially 41, who argues that democrats' views can be inferred from their critics. Jones explicitly excludes drama from political discourse (42 n. 2). Ober, *Mass and Elite*, 19-20 argues for political theory as a critical response to democratic practice, and especially the intellectual problem that stable democracy presented; see also his *Athenian Revolution*, 10-12, and *Political Dissent*. Ober plays down the democratic implications of Protagorean theory (*Athenian Revolution* 129, in criticism of Farrar) on the grounds that it is too difficult to disentangle from Plato (see further below); the difficulties of reconstruction do not, however, exclude the existence of such theory. It is striking how accounts of Greek political thought (see also Ahrensdorf, Euben and Saxonhouse) emphasise critique or downplay specifically democratic foundations. For reflections of democratic theory see n. 30 below, and in general Balot, 48-85, who, however, still argues for a lack of systematic thought.

3. For Ephialtes' reforms and the transition to an activist and fully participatory and deliberative democracy, see Chapter 1. Contemporary theoretical explorations of radical democracy stem largely from the work of Laclau and Mouffe (see also Mouffe, *The Return of the Political*); for a practical application of their approach, see M.P. Brown. A more empirical impetus comes from developments in South America. Van Cott makes the observation, pertinent for the early to mid-fifth century, that the development of 'bottom-up' radical democracy where institutions are weak is particularly well served by strong leadership by individuals.

4. See also 5.302-4, 12.447-9, 20.285-7.

5. For various interpretations, see Solmsen, 83 n. 23. West on *Works and Days* 96 discusses the apparent confusion and suggests (following

Friedlander) that Hesiod is adapting an earlier version where good things flew out of the jar (cf. Babrius, *Fables*. 58; *Anthologia Palatina* 10.71). Griffith on *Prometheus Bound* 250 suggests that in Hesiod 'Hope seems to be a blessing withheld from men so that their life should be the more dreary and depressing'.

6. Bloch, for one, situated all utopian thought under the rubric of the 'principle of hope'.

7. See, e.g., Solon fr. 35. For Solon and hope, see Solmsen, 110-12.

8. Plato's *Gorgias* 523d seems to revisit *Prometheus Bound*: Prometheus is sent by Zeus to take away from mortals knowledge of the day of their death in order to guarantee Zeus' justice, in the judgement of mortals after death. For an account of human development where humans give up for psychological reasons, see Aristophanes' speech on love in Plato's *Symposium* 191a-b.

9. Pindar, *Pythian* 8.95-6; Homer, *Odyssey* 11.207-8; cf. Homer, *Iliad* 6.146-9 (generations like leaves).

10. Compare, for example, Alcman 1.45-59 *PMG*. *Khlidê* has connotations of both luxury and extravagance.

11. Thus Hierokles in *Peace* 1052-1126; Lampon in Eupolis, *Khrysoun Genos* (*Golden Race*) fr. 319, Kratinos, *Drapetides* fr. 62, *Nemesis* fr. 125; Aristophanes, *Clouds* 332, *Birds* 521; religious professionals in general in *Birds* 862-94, 959-90; political oracles in *Knights*, especially 109-222, 997-1110. For Hierokles in a political role, see *IG* I^3 40.64-9 = ML 52; Olson on *Peace* 1045-7; for Lampon, Thucydides 5.19.2, 5.24.1. For discussion, see Bowden and R.C.T. Parker, *Polytheism and Society*, 112-13, 116-18.

12. As famously in the instance of Croesus and the Delphic oracle in Hdt. I.53 with 1.86.1, but compare also Oedipus' over-confidence in *Oedipus Tyrannus*. Teiresias in *Antigone* 998-1022 is closer to Promethean certainties.

13. The placing of bronze before iron may be simply for metrical reasons.

14. See Kleingünther; Cole, 6-7; examples collected by Griffith on 450-506.

15. For Xenophanes, see especially Lesher; for Xenophanes and *Prometheus Bound*, see Conacher, 'Prometheus as Founder of the Arts', 193-4; more sceptically, Stoessl, *Der Prometheus*, 81-2.

16. See fr. 19 for awareness of Thales.

17. There are some ambiguities over the precise nature of Xenophanes' notion of the divine, since there are moments where he seems to admit pluralities of gods too (frr. 1, 23). For discussion of Xenophanes' theology, see Jaeger, 38-54, Eisenstadt and A. Finkelberg, 'Studies in Xenophanes' with bibliography. Likewise, for an emphasis on the ambiguities in Heraclitus' apparently negative presentation of religious ritual, see C. Osborne.

18. For fr. 18, see Tulin, with bibliography. M.J. O'Brien doubts that there is a doctrine of 'primeval brutishness' in Xenophanes, Aeschylus or *Prometheus Bound*. He is clearly wrong on *Prometheus Bound* (see, e.g., Tulin, 38 n. 48) and his linguistic arguments against Xenophanes around the term *thêriôdês* and cognates are hardly decisive.

19. See Griffith, *Authenticity*, 222-3, Griffith, 'Sicily', 111-16, cf. Rösler, 49-55. Bees, 124-5, Lefèvre, 153-5 and Irby-Massie, 143-51 are more optimistic.

20. For medical imagery in *Prometheus Bound*, see Griffith, *Prometheus Bound*, 20-1, Fowler, 174-81 and Petrounias, 98-108.

21. See also *On Ancient Medicine* 7. For the date of this treatise, see Schiefsky, 63-4.

22. See Euripides, *Suppliant Women* 195-218 (late 420s); tr. adesp. fr. 470 (a Palamedes fragment); Kritias, fr. 19 (= fr. 25 D-K). The *Homeric Hymn to Hephaistos* has Hephaistos in the Prometheus role (3-4 recall *Prometheus Bound* 452-3). Pherekrates' *Wild Men* (*Agrioi*) of 420 seems to be sending up this principle.

23. 68 B 5.1 D-K. See Vlastos; Guthrie, *In the Beginning*, 88, 95-9; Cole.

24. = Demokritos fr. 5.1. For the development of language in progressive accounts, see Gera, 112-81.

25. Literally 'separated out' the arts. For a Demokritean origin, see Vlastos and Cole, especially 56-9, with references. An elaboration of this account of human progress is given by Lucretius, *On the Nature of the Universe* 5.925-1457, through an Epicurean filter.

26. For Protagoras' dates, see Plato, *Protagoras* 317b (old enough to be Sokrates' father; Sokrates born in 469); Plato, *Meno* 91d (died at nearly 70, after teaching for forty years or more; cf. Apollodorus *FGH* 244 F 71 = Diogenes Laertius 9.56; Diogenes also gives another version that he lived to 90 (9.55)); he is described as being alive still in Eupolis' *Flatterers* (*Kolakes*; 422/1 BCE).

27. For Protagoras, see Guthrie, *HGP*, III.60-8, 262-9; Kerferd, especially 18-23, 42-4, 131-8, 142-8, 164-8; C.C.W. Taylor, especially 76-84; for his epistemology, Lee, 1-45.

28. Plato's Protagoras does not say whether this was true or false, in line with his agnostic theology; the story assumes Zeus, Athena, Hephaistos and Prometheus, but he is clear that this is a *mythos* (allegory) not a *logos* (argument).

29. The term is impossible to translate adequately in English. For a full study, see Cairns.

30. The only rival is Aeschylus' *Suppliant Women*, although there is more of a display of democracy than a clearly articulated argument for democracy. After Protagoras, the next major arguments for democracy are those of Otanes in Herodotos' debate on the constitutions (3.80.2-6) and the funeral speech by Perikles in Thucydides 2.35-46.

31. M.L. West, 'The Prometheus Trilogy', 148.

32. For discussion, see Griffith, *Sophocles: Antigone*, 180-1, with bibliography.

33. For further studies, see Griffith, *Authenticity*, 217-21, cf. Bees, 248-50, Said, 83-92, Marzullo, Lefèvre, 121-6.

34. Just as, in a more contentious fashion, Protagoras argues in *Protagoras* 316c-317c.

4. Making a Spectacle

1. *tetarton †oês†*. Bywater printed *opsis*, which fits 1453b1-11. The four types of epic at 1459b7-9, however, suggest that the fourth type, albeit out of sequence, should be 'simple' (*haploun* or *haplê*), as Kaibel (in his apparatus) and Lucas (on 1455b32) argue. Either would fit *Prometheus Bound*, but, either way, the categories of the *Poetics* are somewhat confused. See also Lucas on 1456a2. Schrader's emendation, *teratôdes* ('monstrous'), is tempting.

2. *Phorkides (Daughters of Phorkys)* was probably part of a Perseus-related tetralogy (see Gantz, 149-51, cf. Sommerstein, *Aeschylean Tragedy*, 38). Plays on *Ixion* and *Sisyphos* were situated in Hades too, although others also wrote on these characters. We do not know of any non-Aeschylean tragedies on Prometheus.

3. *Life of Aeschylus* 29-30, 55-8 Page; for the *Eumenides* anecdote see 35-8. For Aeschylean grandstanding, see Aristophanes, *Frogs* 907-20, 961-3.

4. Particularly after Taplin, *Stagecraft* and *Greek Tragedy in Action*.

5. See Goette for the classical theatre; Wycherley, 203-14 is fuller and still useful; see also Travlos, 537-52.

6. See Pöhlmann; Goette.

7. In *Agamemnon*, Klytaimestra, Agamemnon and Kassandra are on stage together; *Libation Bearers* requires three characters in most scenes, although Pylades only speaks late in the play; in *Eumenides*, Apollo, Athena and Orestes are simultaneously on stage.

8. For discussion, see Taplin, *Stagecraft*, 325-7, who marginally prefers the use of mute stagehands.

9. For both devices, see in general Taplin, *Stagecraft*, 442-7; for the crane and *skênê* roof, see Mastronarde, 'Actors on High'.

10. There are better arguments, but see, generally, Griffith, 'Sicily'.

11. For evidence relating to the audience, see Pickard-Cambridge, 23-78, Csapo and Slater, 286-305; for discussion, Henderson and Goldhill, 'Representing Democracy'.

12. The entrance-fee is the cornerstone of the argument of Sommerstein, 'The Theatre Audience', for a conservative theatre in the 460s and beyond.

13. For discussion of the punishment see Dyson with bibliography. Dyson further suggests that the bands are fastened through Prometheus in places other than the chest, referring to Cicero's version of *Prometheus Unbound* for multiple spikes, although that is far from conclusive.

14. Basel, Antikenmuseum BS415; see Taplin, *Pots and Plays*, 29 and fig. 8.

15. Davidson, 34-6 argues for a central presence either at the *thymelê* (an altar, not archaeologically attested) or portable scenery. A very minority view has Prometheus on the upper level, but on this see Mastronarde, 'Actors on High', 285.

16. See Hammond, 'Conditions of Production', with elaboration in Hammond, 'More on Conditions of Production'. For criticism, see Davidson, 33. Hammond's suggestion is accepted by M.L. West, 'The Prometheus Trilogy', 136.

17. The reasoning, such as it is, is partly for spectacle, partly to reduce on-stage speaking actors to two. See, however, Taplin, *Stagecraft*, 243-5, with references.

18. Apulian calyx-krater, *c.* 340, attributed to the Branca Painter; Berlin, Antikensammlung, 1969.9 (Taplin, *Pots and Plays*, 81 and fig. 18; Trendall and Webster, III.1.27).

19. Fowler, 181-3; Mossman, 62-6; Petrounias, 108-14; Griffith, *Prometheus Bound*, 21.

20. Most of these examples are included by Taplin, *Stagecraft*, 41-2 in his limited account of spectacular Aeschylean devices, from which he dissociates those of *Prometheus Bound*.

21. Cf. Griffith ad loc., citing Paley.

22. See the discussion of Mastronarde, 'Actors on High': some of his pairs are more convincing than others.

23. For evidence on the chorus, see Pickard-Cambridge, 232-52, and Csapo and Slater, 342-68.

24. Multiple vehicles on a single crane are suggested by Fraenkel, endorsed by Lloyd-Jones, 'Zeus, Prometheus, and Greek Ethics', 57; *six* cranes each with a payload of two are suggested by M.L. West, 'The Prometheus Trilogy', 137-9, modifying Fraenkel's analysis to an even more implausible end.

25. Notably by Griffith, *Prometheus Bound*, 109, Mastronarde, 'Actors on High', 266-8, and now Sommerstein, *Aeschylean Tragedy*, 222-3, but see Taplin, *Stagecraft*, 254-7, and M.L. West, 'The Prometheus Trilogy', 137.

26. Fraenkel, in relation to an aerial entry on the *mêkhanê*.

27. Compiègne 975; *ABV* 331.13: Hammond and Moon, 375-6.

28. See, e.g., the comments of M.L. West, 'The Prometheus Trilogy', 136-7. The comic potential is, to my mind, the danger, but I am skewed by memories of the 1970s children's programme *Chorlton and the*

Wheelies (1976-9). Taplin, *Stagecraft*, 253 doubts any wheeled ground-level entrance.

29. So G. Thomson, 160-1, cf. his note on 130, followed by Davidson, 36 and n. 23, with the important proviso that we do not need to imagine, with Thomson, sea-horses.

30. On the language of ease of movement associated with the chorus, see Fineberg.

31. Griffith, *Prometheus Bound,* 109. Similarly, Taplin, *Stagecraft*, 255-6 objects to the specific mention of a seat.

32. For the 'rule of thumb', see Taplin, *Stagecraft*, 28-39; for discussion and further bibliography, see Revermann, *Comic Business,* 46-65.

33. Likewise, the theatre was evidently not flooded for Arkhippos' *Fishes*.

34. On 286; see Griffith *ad loc.* For the *mêkhanê* here, see Taplin, *Stagecraft*, 260-2; alternative views are collected by Davidson, n. 28.

35. The nickname for the crane, fig-branch (*kradê*), suggests quite a whippy movement.

36. The crane arm would have to be that much longer if Prometheus were mid-*orkhêstra*.

37. Taplin, *Stagecraft*, 270-5 opts for an entirely imaginary earthquake. Dunbar, 751 argues for the *bronteion* (thunder-machine) in Aristophanes' *Birds*, especially 1750-1, and *Clouds* 290 (cf. scholia on 292) and here, as tentatively Griffith on 1082-3. For the *bronteion* see Pollux 4.130; the techniques for thunder effects are described at Hero, *On Making Automata* 20.4.

38. The chorus may not utter the final lines of *Trakhiniai* 1275-8: see discussions of Easterling and Davies ad loc. Many of Euripides' plays have highly suspect choral tail-pieces: see Barrett on Euripides' *Hippolytos* 1462-6.

39. Some elaborate mechanical contrivances have been conceived, possibly over the back retaining wall of the *orkhêstra*, but see Taplin, *Stagecraft*, 274.

40. Discussed sympathetically by Taplin, *Stagecraft*, 274-5, with references.

41. So, e.g., Focke, 284-5 and G. Thomson, 174. It is described, rather unfairly, by Taplin, *Stagecraft*, 273, with further references, as a 'half-measure'.

42. And possibly the far west, if the textually suspect 425-30 is a mangled version of some genuine original text rather than an interpolation.

43. See Hippokrates, *Airs, Waters, Places* 17-22, especially 18; Herodotos 4.1-31, 46-57, correcting earlier accounts, especially Aristeas and Hekataios; Strabo 11.6.2, attacking earlier accounts. See the discussion of Asheri et al., 545-65.

44. *Life of Aeschylus* 85-8 Page.

45. North: Griffith, *Prometheus Bound*, followed by M. Finkelberg, 'The Geography of the *Prometheus Vinctus*', 119-25 (who argues that the instructions to Io are a later interpolation), both of whom put Prometheus in the (far) north-west, which is not essential. South: Bolton, 50-1.

46. Although *Prometheus Bound* misplaces the river Salmydessos from Thrace in the process.

47. Hesychius, *q.v.*; scholia to Apollonius of Rhodes 1.1321, 2.375. For the other version, see Hekataios fr. 203; Herodotos 1.28; Xenophon, *Anabasis* 4.5.34, 4.6.5; Strabo 11.14.5.

48. Kratinos, fr. 343, from an unknown play, and likely to have this passage in mind (so Bakola, 162-3) or perhaps Aeschylus' *Phorkides*, where both sets of sisters appeared (fr. 262). For the traditional location of the Gorgons, see Hesiod, *Theogony* 274-5; Homer and Aristophanes appear to have them in the underworld (*Odyssey* 11.633-5, *Frogs* 475-8). Aeschylus has three Graiai, like the Attic mythographer Pherekydes (fr. 11), rather than the two of *Theogony* 273 (with West ad loc.); Pherekydes, however, keeps the Phorkides separate from his Gorgons.

49. See Bolton, 63, and generally 46-70.

50. On the Greeks in Egypt, see Boardman, 111-53.

51. Herodotos 2.143, cf. 2.15.1; Asheri et al., 231; S.R. West, 'Herodotus' Portrait of Hecataeus'.

52. In Aristophanes' *Akharnians*; that has been doubted by Fornara, 'Date of Herodotus' Publication', who prefers a date *c.* 414, in the light of *Birds* 1127-9 in particular.

53. See, for example, Buxton.

54. The basic implication of *eoikas*, as elsewhere in Hermes' comments, is visual, although it has wider application.

55. Rosenmeyer, 'Tragedy or Treatise?', 100 suggests that it 'verges on exhibitionism'.

56. M.L. West, 'The Prometheus Trilogy', 132 argues that the skulking Prometheus is a visual parody of *Prometheus Fire-bearer* (in the theft of fire), but wrongly downplays comic inventiveness.

5. The Radical Tradition

1. For Varro, see M.L. West, 'The Prometheus Trilogy', 141 n. 66.

2. For general treatments of the Prometheus theme, see Trousson, Duchemin and Dougherty; cf. also Kerenyi.

3. See Philemon fr. 93.1-3.

4. Likewise Horace, *Odes* 1.3, 1.16; Catullus, 64.294; Propertius, 3.5, 2.1; see also Martial 10.39.4; Valerius Flaccus 4.58-81; Juvenal 4.135, 15.84. For artistic representations in Italy, see Raggio, 46 and figures.

5. On all this, see Raggio.

6. For the manuscript tradition, see M.L. West, *Studies*, 319-54; for early editions and translations, see Gruys and Mund-Dopchie, cf. M.L. West, *Studies*, 357-66, and Blasina, 12-16. I am leaving out of account here the heavily abridged/reworked translation of Coriolano Martirano (1556).

7. Raggio, 57.

8. Gruys, 128-33 with bibliography.

9. See Studer and Barbour.

10. Much of *Samson Agonistes* may, however, have been composed before *Paradise Lost*.

11. Prometheus: *Prolusions* III and VII (the latter directly or indirectly derives from Lucian); Aeschylus: preface to *Samson Agonistes*. Milton's treatise, *Pro populo Anglicano Defensio* (*Defence of the People of England*, 1651), quotes from Aeschylus (*Suppliant Women*), Euripides (*Suppliant Women* and *Children of Herakles*) and Sophokles (*Oedipus Tyrannus* and *Antigone*) to make the case for the sovereignty of the people over a king (Patterson, VII.306-12; Dzelzainis, 163-5).

12. For scepticism, see Maxwell.

13. For a (less antagonistic) exploration of the relationship between the Adam and Prometheus myths, see Kreitzer.

14. In *The Marriage of Heaven and Hell*, c. 1790-3 (Keynes, 150).

15. Especially in *Eikonoklastes* (1649).

16. See especially Hill.

17. The Hesiodic myth is no less misogynistic than the Judaeo-Christian, but differently expressed.

18. See, generally, W.R. Parker, *Milton's Debt*, with pp. 177-85 on *Prometheus Bound*.

19. For the pair, see Brewer, albeit rather oversimplified: see W.R. Parker, 184-5.

20. *Samson Agonistes* 184-6 is a plausible echo of *Prometheus Bound* 377-8.

21. See generally *Paradise Lost* VII.126-30, cf. VIII.188-97.

22. Lennox.

23. For Italian translations, see Blasina, 15; for Brumoy, Le Franc de Pompignan and La Porte du Theil, see Macintosh, with bibliography, cf. Trousson, 185-6; for the English translations, see Walton, 40, 108, 198, 208; cf. Hardwick, 'Placing Prometheus'.

24. See, generally, Trousson, 222-9; for poetic traditions and rediscovery of Aeschylus in England, see Kreutz, 7-31.

25. Discussion by Duchemin, 119-29; fuller discussion of Goethe and contemporaries in Trousson, 231-91. Also important are Johann Gottfried von Herder, especially his *der entfesselte Prometheus* (*Prometheus Unbound*) of 1802, and a poem of 1797 by August Wilhelm Schlegel.

26. Jølle, with bibliography.

27. On Romantic and post-Romantic versions, see Bertagnolli.

28. See Trousson, 311-20.

29. Byron had not read Aeschylus since school; the anecdote is recorded by Medwin, 156. See generally Kreutz, 32-80; Dougherty, 104-8, emphasises the Napoleonic allegory.

30. See especially Lewis, 111-55.

31. Presented in the 'Gothic Nightmares' exhibition at Tate Britain in 2006: see Myrone. A detail from an engraving by Fuseli is on the cover of this book.

32. See Junker. Dougherty, 118-21, discusses some twentieth-century art-works.

33. See in general Kreutz, 81-135, Trousson, 321-34 and Lewis, 156-91.

34. Reiman and Powers, 133.

35. By a commentator on Statius, *Thebaid* 4.516, miswriting *demiurgon*: see Pfeiffer, 21-2. Thence, via Boccaccio in particular, he played a number of notable literary cameo roles, such as in Spenser, *The Faerie Queene* I.i.37.8, I.v.22.5, IV.ii.47.7; Marlowe's *Dr. Faustus* I.iii.18; and *Paradise Lost* II.965. Lewis, 185-7, is slightly unreliable here.

36. Kreutz, 122-3.

37. Pollin emphasises the Ovidian Prometheus; Hustis is more rounded, and emphasises Aeschylean compassion. See also Gilbert, 'Horror's Twin'.

38. See *The Quarterly Review* 22 (July 1819), 1-34; see Butler, 236.

39. See also ch. II (Butler, 207) and ch. XXI (Butler, 226).

40. See the references in Kreutz, 83-4. Polidori gives the date for the ghost stories as 15 June 1816 at the Villa Diodati. Byron's *Prometheus* is dated to July 1816 at the same venue.

41. Aldiss, 7-39; cf. Donawerth. Other historians of science fiction disagree: Suvin, 75, for example, puts the genesis of science fiction back into antiquity, but dates the science-fiction novel in the second half of the nineteenth century.

42. As well as more direct uses, such as Aldiss' *Frankenstein Unbound*.

43. Prometheus is the name of the space station where the action takes place in *Solaris*. For *We*, see McCarthy.

44. For Melville, see Woodson, cf. Pachmuss. For Gide, see Duchemin, 162-8, who also discusses other late nineteenth-century (145-61) and early twentieth-century (169-79) French receptions. For the post-Romantic period, see generally Trousson, 387-448. Some post-Romantic American Prometheans are discussed by Riggs.

45. See Gilbert, 'Milton's Bogey', Lewis, 192-201.

46. So, e.g., Thoreau – see Kaiser. Fragments were translated by

Gerard Manley Hopkins but not published until much later; Prometheus can be seen in a number of his works: see Humiliata, Bender, 56-7, K. O'Brien.

47. Falk; Drummond.

48. See Hardwick, 'Placing Prometheus'.

49. 'Socialism Utopian and Scientific', in Marx and Engels, 24.281-325. For a poetic visitor's imagining of Prometheus and the new Soviet system, see Lehmann, 243-55; for a later Eastern bloc Prometheus, see Calder.

50. See, for example, F.L. Smith, 'Prometheus Bound: Technology Mandates Halt Progress'. One work on corporate social responsibility begins, 'Why Prometheus? Because he incarnates the creative entrepreneur who brings to mankind material progress ...' (De Woot, 1). Examples could be multiplied. For a hostile critique of the capitalist Prometheus see Mitzman, especially 91-117. For techno-libertarianism, note in particular the Prometheus Awards from the Libertarian Futurist Society for libertarian fiction instituted by the writer L. Neil Smith, who has an entertaining assault on 'liberals' in the name of Prometheus and progress (*'Prometheus Bound – and Gagged'*).

51. The database of the Archive for the Performance of Greek and Roman Drama as of 21 May 2011 contained 183 entries for *Prometheus Bound*, compared to 872 for *Agamemnon*, 557 for *Libation Bearers* and 510 for *Eumenides*.

52. Especially in *Birth of Tragedy* (1872), §9 (Colli and Montinari, III.I.60-7); for summary and discussion, see Silk and Stern, 71-2, 161-2, 225-96.

53. See the discussions of MacKinnon, 43-8; Wiles, 183-9, van Steen, 'Circular Stage', all with bibliography.

54. Vos, who also references the methods of the Living Theatre group, whose own *Prometheus* was to emerge a decade later: see Berkowitz; Beck et al.; Living Theatre.

55. See van Steen, 'Censors' Rules?'.

56. Galeyev.

57. Paulin; Lowell; both discussed in Hardwick, 'Placing Prometheus'; for Paulin, see also McDonald and Walton, 54-8.

58. Harrison, xxvii.

59. In this respect I agree with the more enthusiastic readings of the film, such as Hall and Dougherty, 124-41; there is a more balanced assessment in Hardwick, 'Placing Prometheus'. For an interesting discussion of post-industrial community theatre in terms of nostalgia, see Brady.

Bibliography

Ahrensdorf, P. J., *Greek Tragedy and Political Philosophy: Rationalism and Religion in Sophocles' Theban Plays* (Cambridge: Cambridge University Press, 2009).

Aldiss, B.W., *Billion Year Spree: The History of Science Fiction* (London: Weidenfeld & Nicolson, 1973).

Allen, D.J., *The World of Prometheus: The Politics of Punishing in Democratic Athens* (Princeton: Princeton University Press, 2000).

Asheri, D., Lloyd, M. and Corcella, A. (eds), *A Commentary on Herodotus Books I-IV* (Oxford: Oxford University Press, 2007).

Bakola, E., *Cratinus and the Art of Comedy* (Oxford: Oxford University Press, 2009).

Balot, R.K., *Greek Political Thought* (Malden, Mass./Oxford, 2006).

Barbour, R., 'Remarkable Ingratitude: Bacon, Prometheus, Democritus', *Studies in English Literature, 1500-1900* 32.1 (1992), 79-90.

Barnes, J. (tr.), *Early Greek Philosophy*, new edn (London: Penguin, 2002).

Barrett, W.S. (tr.), *Euripides: Hippolytus* (Oxford: Clarendon Press, 1964).

Beck, J., Malina, J. and Amitin, M., 'The Living Theatre Abroad: Radicalizing the Classics. Interview with Julian Beck and Judith Malina', *Performing Arts Journal* 5.2 (1981), 26-40.

Bees, R., *Zur Datierung des Prometheus Desmotes* (Stuttgart: Teubner, 1993).

Bender, T.K., *Gerard Manley Hopkins: The Classical Background and Critical Reception of his Work* (Baltimore: Johns Hopkins University Press, 1966).

Berkowitz, G.M., 'Review: [untitled]', *Theatre Journal* 32.1 (1980), 118-19.

Bertagnolli, P.A., *Prometheus in Music: Representations of the Myth in the Romantic Era* (Aldershot: Ashgate, 2007).

Blasina, A. (ed.), *Il Prometeo del duca: la prima traduzione Italiana del Prometeo di Eschilo (vat. urb. Lat. 789)* (Amsterdam: Hakkert, 2006).

Bloch, E., *The Principle of Hope* (Oxford: Basil Blackwell, 1986), tr. Neville Plaice, Stephen Plaice and Paul Knight.

Boardman, J., *The Greeks Overseas: Their Colonies and Trade*, 4th edn (London: Thames and Hudson, 1999).

Bolton, J.D.P., *Aristeas of Proconnesus* (Oxford: Clarendon Press, 1962).

Bonner, R.J. and Smith, G., *The Administration of Justice from Homer to Aristotle* (New York: Greenwood Press, 1930-38), 2 vols.

Bowden, H., 'Oracles for Sale', in Derow, P. and Parker, R.C.T. (eds.), *Herodotus and his World* (Oxford: Oxford University Press, 2003), 256-74.

Brady, S., 'Welded to the Ladle: *Steelbound* and Non-Radicality in Community-Based Theatre', *Drama Review* 44.3 (2000), 51-74.

Brewer, W., 'Two Athenian Models for *Samson Agonistes*', *Proceedings of the Modern Language Association* 42.4 (1927), 910-20.

Brown, A.L., '*Prometheus Pyrphoros*', *Bulletin of the Institute of Classical Studies* 37 (1990), 50-6.

Brown, M.P., *RePlacing Citizenship: AIDS Activism and Radical Democracy* (New York/London: Guilford Press, 1997).

Burian, P., 'Greek Tragedy as Democratic Discourse', in D.M. Carter (ed.), *Why Athens?*, 95-117.

Butler, M., *Mary Shelley: Frankenstein, or the Modern Prometheus. The 1818 text* (Oxford: Oxford University Press, 1994).

Buxton, R.G.A., 'Blindness and Limits: Sophokles and the Logic of Myth', *Journal of Hellenic Studies* 100 (1980), 22-37.

Cairns, D.L., *Aidôs: The Psychology and Ethics of Honour and Shame in Ancient Greek Literature* (Oxford: Clarendon Press, 1993).

Calder, W.M., 'Aeschylus, Prometheus: a DDR interpretation', in Faber, R. and Seidensticker, B. (eds), *Worte, Bilder, Töne: Studien zur Antike und Antikerezeption Bernhard Kytzler zu ehren* (Würzburg: Königshausen und Neumann, 1996), 323-9.

Carter, D.M., *The Politics of Greek Tragedy* (Exeter: Bristol Phoenix Press, 2007).

Carter, D.M., *Why Athens? A Reappraisal of Tragic Politics* (Oxford: Oxford University Press, 2011).

Carter, L. B., *The Quiet Athenian* (Oxford: Clarendon Press, 1986).

Cole, A. T., *Democritus and the Sources of Greek Anthropology* (Cleveland: American Philological Association, 1967).

Collard, C. (tr.), *Aeschylus: Persians and Other Plays* (Oxford: Oxford University Press, 2009).

Colli, G. and Montinari, M. (eds), *Friedrich Nietzsche: Werke* (Berlin: de Gruyter, 1967-).

Conacher, D.J., 'Prometheus as Founder of the Arts', *Greek, Roman and Byzantine Studies* 18 (1977), 189-206.

Bibliography

Conacher, D. J., *Aeschylus' Prometheus Bound: A Literary Commentary* (Toronto: University of Toronto Press, 1980).

Csapo, E. and Slater, W.J., *The Context of Ancient Drama* (Ann Arbor: University of Michigan Press, 1995).

Davidson, J., '*Prometheus Vinctus* on the Athenian Stage', *Greece and Rome* 41.1 (1994), 33-40.

Davies, J.K., 'Demosthenes on Liturgies: a Note', *Journal of Hellenic Studies* 87 (1967), 33-40.

Davies, J.K., *Democracy and Classical Greece*, 2nd edn (London: Fontana, 1993).

Davison, J.A., 'The Date of the *Prometheia*', *Transactions and Proceedings of the American Philological Association* 80 (1949), pp. 66-93.

Davison, J.A., 'Aeschylus and Athenian Politics, 472-456 BC', in Badian, E. (ed.), *Ancient Society and Institutions: Studies Presented to Victor Ehrenberg on his 75th Birthday* (Oxford: Blackwell, 1966), 93-107.

Dodds, E.R., *The Ancient Concept of Progress, and Other Essays on Greek Literature and Belief* (Oxford: Clarendon Press, 1973).

Dodds, E.R., 'The *Prometheus Vinctus* and the Progress of Scholarship', in Dodds, *Progress*, 26-44.

Dodds, E.R., 'Morals and Politics in the *Oresteia*', in Dodds, *Progress*, 45-63.

Donawerth, J., *Frankenstein's Daughters: Women Writing Science Fiction* (New York: Syracuse University Press, 1996).

Dougherty, C., *Prometheus* (London: Routledge, 2005).

Dover, K.J., 'The Political Aspects of Aeschylus' *Eumenides*', *Journal of Hellenic Studies* 77 (1957), 230-7.

Drummond, C., 'A "Grand Possible": Elizabeth Barrett Browning's Translations of Aeschylus's "Prometheus Bound"', *International Journal of the Classical Tradition* 12.4 (2006), 507-62.

Dübner, L., *Attische Feste* (Hildesheim: Olms, 1962).

Duchemin, J., *Prométhée: histoire du mythe, de ses origines orientales à ses incarnations modernes* (Paris: Les Belles Lettres, 1974).

Dunbar, N.V. (ed.), *Aristophanes: Birds* (Oxford: Clarendon Press, 1995).

Duncan, H., *Vellum* (London: Pan Macmillan, 2006).

Dyson, M., 'Prometheus and the Wedge: Text and Staging at Aeschylus, *PV* 54-81', *Journal of Hellenic Studies* 114 (1994), 154-6.

Dzelzainis, M. (ed.), *John Milton: Political Writings* (Cambridge: Cambridge University Press, 1990), tr. Claire Gruzelier.

Easterling, P.E. (ed.), *The Cambridge Companion to Greek Tragedy* (Cambridge: Cambridge University Press, 1997).

Easterling, P.E., 'Anachronism in Greek Tragedy', *Journal of Hellenic Studies* 105 (1985), 1-10.

Bibliography

Eisenstadt, M., 'Xenophanes' Proposed Reform of Greek Religion', *Hermes* 102.2 (1974), 142-50.

Euben, J.P., *The Tragedy of Political Theory: The Road Not Taken* (Ithaca/London: Cornell University Press, 1990).

Ewans, M., 'Prometheus Bound', *Ramus* 6 (1977), 1-14.

Falk, A., 'Elizabeth Barrett Browning and Her Prometheuses: Self-Will and a Woman Poet', *Tulsa Studies in Women's Literature* 7.1 (1988), 69-85.

Farnell, L.R., 'The Paradox of the *Prometheus Vinctus*', *Journal of Hellenic Studies* 53 (1933), 40-50.

Farrar, C., *The Origins of Democratic Thinking: The Invention of Politics in Classical Athens* (Cambridge: Cambridge University Press, 1988).

Fineberg, S., 'The Unshod Maidens at *Prometheus* 135', *American Journal of Philology* 107.1 (1986), 95-8.

Finkelberg, A., 'Studies in Xenophanes', *Harvard Studies in Classical Philology* 93 (1990), 103-67.

Finkelberg, M., 'The Geography of the *Prometheus Vinctus*', *Rheinisches Museum* 141.2 (1998), 119-41.

Flintoff, E., 'Aristophanes and the *Prometheus Bound*', *Classical Quarterly* 33.1 (1983), 1-5.

Flintoff, E., 'The Date of the *Prometheus Bound*', *Mnemosyne* 39.1/2 (1986), 82-91.

Focke, F., 'Aischylos' Prometheus', *Hermes* 65.3 (1930), 259-304.

Foley, H.P., 'Choral Identity in Greek Tragedy', *Classical Philology* 98.1 (2003), 1-30.

Fornara, C.W., 'Evidence for the Date of Herodotus' Publication', *Journal of Hellenic Studies* 91 (1971), 24-34.

Fornara, C.W., *Archaic Times to the End of the Peloponnesian War*, Translated Documents of Greece and Rome 1 (Cambridge: Cambridge University Press, 1983).

Forrest, W.G.G., 'Themistocles and Argos', *Classical Quarterly* 10 (1960), 221-41.

Forrest, W.G.G., *The Emergence of Greek Democracy: The Character of Greek Politics, 800-400 BC* (London: Weidenfeld & Nicolson, 1966).

Fowler, B.H., 'The Imagery of the *Prometheus Bound*', *American Journal of Philology* 78.2 (1957), 173-84.

Fraenkel, E., 'Der Einzug des Chors im *Prometheus*', *Annali della Scuola Normale Superiore di Pisa, Cl. di Lettere e Filosofia* 23 (1954), 269-84, reprinted in *Kleine Beiträge zur klassischen Philologie* (Rome: Edizioni di storia e letteratura), I.389-406.

Gagarin, M., *Aeschylean Drama* (University of California Press: Berkeley, 1976).

Gagarin, M. and Woodruff, P. (trs), *Early Greek Political Thought from*

Bibliography

Homer to the Sophists (Cambridge: Cambridge University Press, 1995).

Galeyev, B.M., 'The Fire of Prometheus: Music-Kinetic Art Experiments in the USSR', *Leonardo* 21.4 (1988), 383-96.

Gantz, T., 'The Aischylean Tetralogy: Attested and Conjectured Groups', *American Journal of Philology* 101 (1980), 133-64.

Garvie, A.F., *Aeschylus' Supplices: Play and Trilogy*, 2nd edn (Exeter: Bristol Phoenix Press, 2006).

Garvie, A.F. (ed.), *Aeschylus: Persae* (Oxford: Oxford University Press, 2009).

Gera, D.L., *Ancient Greek Ideas on Speech, Language and Civilization* (Oxford: Oxford University Press, 2003).

Gilbert, S.M., 'Horror's Twin: Mary Shelley's Monstrous Eve', *Feminist Studies* 4.2 (1978), 48-73.

Gilbert, S.M., 'Patriarchal Poetry and Women Readers: Reflections on Milton's Bogey', *Proceedings of the Modern Language Association* 93.3 (1978), 368-82.

Goette, H.R., 'An Archaeological Appendix', in Wilson, P. J. (ed.), *The Greek Theatre and Festivals: Documentary Studies* (Oxford: Clarendon Press, 2007), 116-21.

Golden, L., *In Praise of Prometheus: Humanism and Rationalism in Aeschylean Thought* (Chapel Hill: University of North Carolina Press, 1966).

Goldhill, S., *Reading Greek Tragedy* (Cambridge: Cambridge University Press, 1986).

Goldhill, S., 'The Great Dionysia and Civic Ideology', *Journal of Hellenic Studies* 107 (1987), 56-76. A revised version appears in Winkler & Zeitlin, 87-129.

Goldhill, S., 'Representing Democracy: Women at the Great Dionysia', in Osborne, R.G. and Hornblower, S. (eds), *Ritual, Finance, Politics: Athenian Democratic Accounts Presented to D.M. Lewis* (Oxford: Clarendon Press, 1994), 347-69.

Goldhill, S., 'Collectivity and Otherness – The Authority of the Tragic Chorus: Response to Gould', in Silk, *Tragedy and the Tragic*, 244-56.

Gomme, A.W., Andrewes, A. and Dover, K.J., *A Historical Commentary on Thucydides* (Oxford: Clarendon Press, 1945-81), 5 vols.

Gould, J., 'Tragedy and Collective Experience', in Silk, *Tragedy and the Tragic*, 217-43.

Gregory, J. (ed.), *A Companion to Greek Tragedy* (Oxford: Blackwell, 2005).

Grene, D. and Lattimore, R. (trs), *Aeschylus* (Chicago: University of Chicago Press, 1956).

Griffith, M., *The Authenticity of Prometheus Bound* (Cambridge: Cambridge University Press, 1977).

Bibliography

Griffith, M., 'Aeschylus, Sicily and Prometheus', in Dawe, R.D., Diggle, J. and Easterling, P.E. (eds), *Dionysiaca: Nine Studies in Greek Poetry by Former Pupils, Presented to Denys Page on his Seventieth Birthday* (Cambridge: Cambridge Faculty Library, 1978), 105-39.

Griffith, M. (ed.), *Aeschylus. Prometheus Bound* (Cambridge: Cambridge University Press, 1983).

Griffith, M. (ed.), *Sophocles: Antigone* (Cambridge: Cambridge University Press, 1999).

Gruys, J.A., *The Early Printed Editions (1518-1664) of Aeschylus: a Chapter in the History of Classical Scholarship, Bibliotheca humanistica & reformatorica* 32 (Nieuwkoop: de Graaf, 1981).

Guthrie, W.K.C., *In the Beginning: Some Greek Views on the Origins of Life and the Early State of Man* (London: Methuen, 1957).

Guthrie, W.K.C., *A History of Greek Philosophy* (Cambridge: Cambridge University Press, 1962-81).

Hall, E., 'Tony Harrison's *Prometheus*: A View from the Left', *Arion* 10.1 (2002), 129-40.

Hammond, N.G.L., 'The Conditions of Production to the Death of Aeschylus', *Greek, Roman and Byzantine Studies* 13.4 (1972), 387-450.

Hammond, N.G.L., 'More on Conditions of Production to the Death of Aeschylus', *Greek, Roman and Byzantine Studies* 29.1 (1988), 5-33.

Hammond, N.G.L. and Moon, W.G., 'Illustrations of Early Tragedy at Athens', *American Journal of Archaeology* 82.3 (1978), 371-83.

Hardwick, L., 'Placing Prometheus', in Hardwick, L. (ed.), *Tony Harrison's Poetry, Drama and Film.*

Hardwick, L. (ed.), *Tony Harrison's Poetry, Drama and Film: the Classical Dimension, Open Colloquium* (Milton Keynes: The Open University, October 1999). www2.open.ac.uk/ClassicalStudies/GreekPlays/Colq99/colq99.htm (last visited 9 February 2012)

Harrison, T., *Prometheus* (London: Faber & Faber, 1998).

Henderson, J., 'Women and the Athenian Dramatic Festivals', *Transactions and Proceedings of the American Philological Association* 121 (1991), 133-47.

Herington, C.J., 'Aeschylus: The Last Phase', *Arion* 4.3 (1965), 387-403.

Herington, C.J., *The Author of the Prometheus Bound* (Austin, Tx.: University of Texas Press, 1970).

Herington, C.J. and Scully, J. (trs), *Aeschylus: Prometheus Bound* (New Haven/London: Yale University Press, 1975).

Hill, C., *Milton and the English Revolution* (London/New York: Faber & Faber, 1977).

Hornblower, S., *A Commentary on Thucydides* (Oxford: Oxford University Press, 1991-2008), 3 vols.

Hornblower, S., *The Greek World, 479-323 BC*, 3rd edn (London: Routledge, 2002).

Hubbard, T. K., 'Recitative Anapests and the Authenticity of *Prometheus Bound*', *American Journal of Philology* 112.4 (1991), 439-60.

Humiliata, M., 'Hopkins and the Prometheus Myth', *Proceedings of the Modern Language Association* 70.1 (1955), 58-68.

Hussey, E., *The Presocratics*, new edn (London: Bristol Classical Press, 1998).

Hustis, H., 'Responsible Creativity and the "Modernity" of Mary Shelley's Prometheus', *Studies in English Literature, 1500-1900* 43.4 (2003), 845-58.

Hutchinson, G.O. (ed.), *Aeschylus, Seven Against Thebes* (Oxford: Clarendon Press, 1985).

Irby-Massie, G., '*Prometheus Bound* and Contemporary Trends in Greek Natural Philosophy', *Greek, Roman and Byzantine Studies* 48.2 (2008), 133-57.

Jaeger, W., *The Theology of the Early Greek Philosophers* (Oxford: Clarendon Press, 1947).

Jens, W. (ed.), *Die Bauformen der griechischen Tragödie* (Munich: Fink, 1971).

Jølle, J., '"Prince poli & savant": Goethe's Prometheus and the Enlightenment', *Modern Language Review* 99.2 (2004), 394-415.

Jones, A.H.M., *Athenian Democracy* (Oxford: Blackwell, 1957).

Junker, P., 'Thomas Cole's "Prometheus Bound:" An Allegory for the 1840s', *American Art Journal* 31.1/2 (2000), 32-55.

Kahn, D., 'Inaros' Rebellion against Artaxerxes I and the Athenian Disaster in Egypt', *Classical Quarterly* 58.2 (2008), 424-40.

Kaiser, L.M., 'Remarks on Thoreau's Translation of the *Prometheus*', *Classical Weekly* 46.5 (1953), 69-70.

Kassel, R. and Austin, C.F. (eds), *Poetae Comici Graeci* (Berlin: de Gruyter, 1983-).

Kerenyi, K., *Prometheus: Archetypal Image of Human Existence* (London: Thames & Hudson, 1963).

Kerferd, G.B., *The Sophistic Movement* (Cambridge: Cambridge University Press, 1981).

Keynes, G. (ed.), *The Complete Writings of William Blake: with Variant Readings*, new edn (Oxford: Oxford University Press, 1966).

Kleingünther, A., *Protos Heuretes: Untersuchungen zur Geschichte einer Fragestellung* (Leipzig: Dieterich, 1933).

Knox, B.M.W., *The Heroic Temper: Studies in Sophoclean Tragedy* (Berkeley/London: University of California Press, 1964).

Kreitzer, L.J., *Prometheus and Adam: Enduring Symbols of the Human Situation* (Lanham, Md.: University Press of America, 1994).

Bibliography

Kreutz, C., *Das Prometheussymbol in der Dichtung der englischen Romantik* (Göttingen: Vandenhoeck & Ruprecht, 1963).

Laclau, E. and Mouffe, C., *Hegemony and Socialist Strategy: Towards a Radical Democratic Politics*, 2nd edn (London: Verso, 2001).

Lavelle, B.M., *The Sorrow and the Pity: A Prolegomenon to a History of Athens under the Peisistratids, c. 560-510 BC, Historia Einzelschriften* 80 (Stuttgart: Steiner, 1993).

Lee, M.-K., *Epistemology After Protagoras: Responses to Relativism in Plato, Aristotle, and Democritus* (Oxford: Oxford University Press, 2005).

Lefèvre, E., *Studien zu den Quellen und zum Verständnis des Prometheus Desmotes* (Göttingen: Vandenhoeck und Ruprecht, 2003).

Lefkowitz, M.R., *The Lives of the Greek Poets* (London: Duckworth, 1981).

Lehmann, J., *Prometheus and the Bolsheviks* (London: Cresset Press, 1937).

Lennox, C. (tr.), *The Greek Theatre of Father Brumoy* (London, 1759).

Lesher, J.H. (ed.), *Xenophanes of Colophon* (Toronto/London: University of Toronto Press, 1992).

Lewis, L.M., *The Promethean Politics of Milton, Blake and Shelley* (Columbia/London: University of Missouri Press, 1992).

Lewis, R.G., 'Themistokles and Ephialtes', *Classical Quarterly* 47.2 (1997), 358-62.

Libertarian Futurist Society, *Prometheus Awards* (2010), http://www.lfs.org/awards.htm (accessed 15 June 2010).

Living Theatre, The, 'The Living Theatre in "Prometheus": A Collective Creation', *Performing Arts Journal* 5.2 (1981), 41-7.

Lloyd-Jones, H., 'Zeus in Aeschylus', *Journal of Hellenic Studies* 76 (1956), 55-67.

Lloyd-Jones, H., *The Justice of Zeus*, 2nd edn (Berkeley/London: University of California Press, 1983).

Lloyd-Jones, H., 'Zeus, Prometheus, and Greek Ethics', *Harvard Studies in Classical Philology* 101 (2003), 49-72.

Long, H. S., 'Notes on Aeschylus' *Prometheus Bound*', *Proceedings of the American Philosophical Society* 102 (1958), 229-80.

Low, P. (ed.), *The Athenian Empire* (Edinburgh: Edinburgh University Press, 2008).

Lowell, R., *Prometheus Bound, derived from Aeschylus* (London: Faber, 1970).

McCarthy, P.A., 'Zamyatin and the Nightmare of Technology (Zamyatine et le cauchemar de la technologie)', *Science Fiction Studies* 11.2 (1984), 122-9.

McDonald, M. and Walton, J.M. (eds), *Amid our Troubles: Irish Versions of Greek Tragedy* (London: Methuen, 2002).

161

Bibliography

Macintosh, F., 'The "Rediscovery" of Aeschylus for the Modern Stage', in Jouanna, J. and Montanari, F. (eds), *Éschyle à l'aube du théâtre occidental: neuf exposés suivis de discussions* (Geneva: Fondation Hardt, 2008), 435-68.

MacKinnon, K., *Greek Tragedy into Film* (Cranbury, N.J.: Associated University Presses, 1986).

Marx, K. and Engels, F., *Collected Works* (London: Lawrence & Wishart, 1975-2005).

Marzullo, B., *I sofismi di Prometeo* (Firenze: La Nuova Italia, 1993).

Mastronarde, D.J., 'Actors on High: The Skene Roof, the Crane, and the Gods in Attic Drama', *Classical Antiquity* 9.2 (1990), 247-94.

Mastronarde, D.J., 'Knowledge and Authority in the Choral Voice of Euripidean Tragedy', *Syllecta Classica* 10 (1999), 87-104.

Mastronarde, D.J., (ed.), *Euripides: Medea* (Cambridge: Cambridge University Press, 2002).

Maxwell, J.C., 'Milton's Knowledge of Aeschylus: The Argument from Parallel Passages', *Review of English Studies* 3.12 (1952), 366-71.

Medwin, T., *Conversations of Lord Byron* (Princeton: Princeton University Press, 1966), ed. Ernest J. Lovell, based on the new edn of 1824.

Meiggs, R., 'The Crisis of Athenian Imperialism', *Harvard Studies in Classical Philology* 67 (1963), 1-36.

Meiggs, R., *The Athenian Empire* (Oxford: Oxford University Press, 1972).

Mitzman, A., *Prometheus Revisited: The Quest for Global Justice in the Twenty-first Century* (Amherst/Boston: University of Massachusetts Press, 2003).

Mossman, J.M., 'Chains of Imagery in *Prometheus Bound*', *Classical Quarterly* 46.1 (1996), 58-67.

Mouffe, C., *The Return of the Political* (London: Verso, 1993).

Mund-Dopchie, M., *La survie d'Eschyle à la Renaissance* (Louvain: Peeters, 1984).

Murray, R.D., *The Motif of Io in Aeschylus' Suppliants* (Princeton: Princeton University Press, 1958).

Myrone, M., *Gothic Nightmares: Fuseli, Blake and the Romantic Imagination* (London: Tate Publishing, 2006).

Ober, J., *Mass and Elite in Democratic Athens: Rhetoric, Ideology, and the Power of the People* (Princeton: Princeton University Press, 1989).

Ober, J., *The Athenian Revolution: Essays on Ancient Greek Democracy and Political Theory* (Princeton: Princeton University Press, 1996).

Ober, J., *Political Dissent in Democratic Athens: Intellectual Critics of Popular Rule* (Princeton: Princeton University Press, 1998).

O'Brien, K., 'Saying Yes at Lightning: The Prometheus/Job Paradigm in Part the First of "The Wreck of the Deutschland"', *Victorian Poetry* 36.3 (1998), 247-58.

O'Brien, M.J., 'Xenophanes, Aeschylus, and the Doctrine of Primeval Brutishness', *Classical Quarterly* 35.2 (1985), 264-77.

Olson, S.D. (ed.), *Aristophanes: Peace* (Oxford: Clarendon Press, 1998).

Osborne, C., 'Heraclitus and the Rites of Established Religion', in A.B. Lloyd (ed.), *What is a God?* (London: Duckworth/Classical Press of Wales, 1997), 35-42.

Osborne, R.G., Hornblower, S. and Greenstock, M.C. (eds.), *The Athenian Empire, LACTOR*, 4th edn (Harrow: London Association of Classical Teachers, 1983).

Pachmuss, T., 'Prometheus and Job Reincarnated: Melville and Dostoevskij', *The Slavic and East European Journal* 23.1 (1979), 25-37.

Page, D.L. (ed.), *Aeschyli septem quae supersunt tragoedias* (Oxford: Clarendon Press, 1972).

Parke, H.W., *Festivals of the Athenians* (London: Thames & Hudson, 1977).

Parker, R.C.T., *Athenian Religion: A History* (Oxford: Clarendon Press, 1996).

Parker, R.C.T., *Polytheism and Society at Athens* (Oxford: Oxford University Press, 2005).

Parker, W.R., *Milton's Debt to Greek Tragedy in Samson Agonistes* (New York: Barnes & Noble, 1969), originally published in 1937.

Patterson, F.A. (ed.), *John Milton: The Works* (New York: Columbia University Press, 1931-1940).

Pattoni, P., *L'autenticità del Prometeo incatenato di Eschilo* (Pisa: Scuola Normale Superiore, 1987).

Paulin, T., *Seize the Fire: a Version of Aeschylus' Prometheus Bound* (London: Faber, 1990).

Petrounias, E., *Funktion und Thematik der Bilder bei Aischylos* (Göttingen: Vandenhoeck & Ruprecht, 1978).

Pfeiffer, I.L. (ed.), *Three Aiginetan Odes of Pindar: a Commentary on Nemean V, Nemean VIII, & Pythian VIII* (Leiden: Brill, 1999).

Pfeiffer, R., *History of Classical Scholarship from 1300 to 1850* (Oxford: Clarendon Press, 1976).

Pickard-Cambridge, A.W., *The Dramatic Festivals of Athens*, 2nd edn (Oxford: Clarendon Press, 1988), revised with addenda by John Gould and D.M. Lewis.

Podlecki, A.J., *The Political Background of Aeschylean Tragedy*, 2nd edn (London: Bristol Classical Press, 1999).

Podlecki, A.J. (ed.), *Aeschylus: Prometheus Bound* (Warminster: Aris and Phillips, 2005).

Pöhlmann, E., 'Die Proedrie des Dionysostheaters im 5. Jahrhundert und das Bühnenspiel der Klassik', *Museum Helveticum* 38 (1983), 129-46.

Bibliography

Pollin, B.R., 'Philosophical and Literary Sources of *Frankenstein*', *Comparative Literature* 17.2 (1965), 97-108.

Raaflaub, K.A., *The Discovery of Freedom in Ancient Greece* (Chicago: Chicago University Press, 2004).

Raggio, O., 'The Myth of Prometheus. Its Survival and Metamorphoses up to the XVIIIth Century', *Journal of the Warburg and Courtauld Institutes* 21 (1958), 44-62.

Reiman, D.H. and Powers, S.B., *Shelley's Poetry and Prose* (New York/London: W.W. Norton, 1977).

Reinhardt, K., *Aischylos als Regisseur und Theologe* (Bern: Francke, 1949).

Revermann, M., 'Cratinus' *Dionysalexandros* and the Head of Pericles', *Journal of Hellenic Studies* 117 (1997), 197-200.

Revermann, M., *Comic Business: Theatricality, Dramatic Technique, and Performance Contexts of Aristophanic Comedy* (Oxford: Oxford University Press, 2006).

Rhodes, P. J., *The Athenian Boule* (Oxford: Clarendon Press, 1972).

Rhodes, P. J., *A Commentary on the Aristotelian Athenaion Politeia*, reprinted with addenda (Oxford: Oxford University Press, 1992).

Rhodes, P. J., 'Nothing to Do with Democracy: Athenian Drama and the Polis', *Journal of Hellenic Studies* 123 (2003), 104-19.

Rhodes, P. J., *A History of the Classical Greek World 478-323 BC* (Malden, Mass./Oxford: Blackwell, 2006).

Riggs, Thomas, J., 'Prometheus 1900', *American Literature* 22.4 (1951), 399-423.

Rihll, T.E., 'Democracy Denied: Why Ephialtes Attacked the Areiopagus', *Journal of Hellenic Studies* 115 (1995), 87-98.

Robertson, D.S., 'On the Chronology of Aeschylus', *Proceedings of the Cambridge Philological Society* 169-71 (1938), 9-10.

Robertson, D.S., 'Prometheus and Chiron', *Journal of Hellenic Studies* 71 (1951), 150-5.

Robinson, E.W., 'Thucydidean Sieges, Prosopitis, and the Hellenic Disaster in Egypt', *Classical Antiquity* 18.1 (1999), 132-52.

Roller, D.W., 'Who Murdered Ephialtes?', *Historia* 38.3 (1989), 257-66.

Rosenmeyer, T.G., '*Prometheus Bound*: Tragedy or Treatise?', in *The Masks of Tragedy: Essays on Six Greek Dramas* (New York: Gordian Press, 1971), 49-102.

Rosenmeyer, T.G., *The Art of Aeschylus* (University of California Press: Berkeley/London, 1982).

Rösler, W., *Reflexe vorsokratischen Denkens bei Aischylos* (Meisenheim am Glan: A. Hain, 1970).

Ruffell, I.A., 'The World Turned Upside Down: Utopia and Utopianism in the Fragments of Old Comedy', in Wilkins, J. and Harvey, D. (eds), *The Rivals of Aristophanes: Studies in Athenian Old Comedy* (London: Duckworth/Classical Press of Wales, 2000), 473-506.

Ruffell, I.A., 'A Total Write-Off: Aristophanes, Cratinus and the Rhetoric of Comic Competition', *Classical Quarterly* 52.1 (2002), 138-63.

Said, S., *Sophiste et tyran: le problème du Prométhée enchaîné* (Paris: Klincksieck, 1985).

Saxonhouse, A.W., *Fear of Diversity: The Birth of Political Science in Ancient Greek Thought* (Chicago and London: University of Chicago Press, 1992).

Schiefsky, M.J. (ed.), *Hippocrates, On Ancient Medicine, translated with introduction and commentary* (Leiden: Brill).

Schmid, W., *Untersuchungen zum gefesselten Prometheus, Tübinger Beiträge zur Altertumswissenschaft* 9 (Stuttgart: Kohlhammer, 1929).

Scott, W.C., 'The Development of the Chorus in *Prometheus Bound*', *Transactions and Proceedings of the American Philological Association* 117 (1987), 85-96.

Sealey, R., 'Ephialtes', *Classical Philology* 59.1 (1964), 11-22.

Sealey, R., 'Ephialtes, *Eisangelia*, and the Council', in Rhodes, P. J. (ed.), *Athenian Democracy* (Edinburgh: Edinburgh University Press, 2004), 310-24.

Silk, M.S. (ed.), *Tragedy and the Tragic: Greek Theatre and Beyond* (Oxford: Clarendon Press, 1996).

Silk, M.S., 'Style, Voice and Authority in the Choruses of Greek Drama', in Riemer, P. and Zimmermann, B. (eds), *Der Chor im antiken und modernen Drama, Drama* 3 (Stuttgart and Weimar: M&P, 1998), 1-26.

Silk, M.S. and Stern, J.P., *Nietzsche on Tragedy* (Cambridge: Cambridge University Press, 1981).

Smith, F.L., 'Prometheus Bound: Technology Mandates Halt Progress', *Regulation (The Cato Review of Business and Government)* 20.1 (1997), http://cato.org/pubs/regulation/regv20n1/reg20n1g. html (accessed 20 August 2010).

Smith, L.N., 'Prometheus Bound and Gagged' (2010), http://www.lneilsmith.org/promethe.html (accessed 15 June 2010). Originally published in *Lever Action: Essays on Liberty* (Mountain Media, 2001).

Snell, B., Radt, S.L. and Kannicht, R. (eds), *Tragicorum Graecorum Fragmenta* (Göttingen: Vandenhoeck & Ruprecht, 1971-2004).

Solmsen, F., *Hesiod and Aeschylus* (Ithaca/London: Cornell University Press, 1949).

Sommerstein, A.H., 'The Theatre Audience, The *Demos* and the *Suppliants* of Aeschylus', in Pelling, C.B.R. (ed.), *Greek Tragedy and the Historian* (Oxford: Clarendon Press, 1997), 63-79.

Sommerstein, A.H. (ed.), *Aeschylus* (Cambridge, Mass.: Harvard University Press, 2009), three volumes.

Sommerstein, A.H., *Aeschylean Tragedy*, 2nd edn (Duckworth: London, 2010).

Sourvinou-Inwood, C., *Tragedy and Athenian Religion* (Lanham, Md.: Lexington Books, 2003).

Stoessl, F., 'Aeschylus as a Political Thinker', *American Journal of Philology* 73.2 (1952), 113-39.

Stoessl, F., *Der Prometheus des Aischylos als geistesgeschichtliches und theatergeschichtliches Phänomen* (Stuttgart: Steiner, 1988).

Studer, H.D., '"Strange Fire at the Altar of the Lord": Francis Bacon on Human Nature', *Review of Politics* 65.2 (2003), 209-35.

Suvin, D., *Positions and Presuppositions in Science Fiction* (Basingstoke: Macmillan, 1988).

Taplin, O.P., *The Stagecraft of Aeschylus* (Oxford: Clarendon Press, 1977).

Taplin, O.P., *Greek Tragedy in Action* (London: Methuen, 1978).

Taplin, O.P., 'Spreading the Word Through Performance', in Goldhill, S. and Osborne, R.G. (eds), *Performance Culture and Athenian Democracy* (Cambridge: Cambridge University Press, 1999), 33-57.

Taplin, O.P., *Pots and Plays: Interactions between Tragedy and Greek Vase-painting of the Fourth Century BC* (Los Angeles: John Paul Getty Museum, 2007).

Taylor, C.C.W. (tr.), *Plato: Protagoras*, rev. edn (Oxford: Clarendon Press, 1991).

Taylor, M.W., *The Tyrant Slayers: The Heroic Image in Fifth Century BC Athenian Art and Politics*, 2nd edn (Salem, N.H.: Ayer, 1991).

Thomson, G. (ed.), *The Prometheus Bound* (Cambridge: Cambridge University Press, 1932).

Thomson, G., 'Notes on *Prometheus Vinctus*', *Classical Quarterly* 23.3/4 (1929), 155-63.

Thomson, G., *Aeschylus and Athens: a Study in the Social Origins of Drama*, 4th edn (London: Lawrence & Wishart, 1973).

Thomson, J.A.K., 'The Religious Background of the *Prometheus Vinctus*', *Harvard Studies in Classical Philology* 31 (1920), 1-37.

Travlos, J., *Pictorial Dictionary of Ancient Athens* (London: Thames and Hudson, 1971).

Trendall, A.D. and Webster, T.B.L., *Illustrations of Greek Drama* (London: Phaidon, 1971).

Trousson, R., *Le Thème de Prométhée dans la littérature européenne*, 2 vols (Geneva: Librairie Droz, 1964).

Tulin, A., 'Xenophanes Fr. 18 D.-K. and the Origins of the Idea of Progress', *Hermes* 121.2 (1993), 129-38.

Unterberger, R., *Der gefesselte Prometheus des Aischylos. Eine Interpretation*, *Tübinger Beiträge zur Altertumswissenschaft* (Stuttgart: Kohlhammer, 1968).

Van Cott, D.L., *Radical Democracy in the Andes* (Cambridge: Cambridge University Press, 2008).

van Steen, G., 'Playing by the Censors' Rules? Classical Drama Revived under the Greek Junta (1967-1974)', *Journal of the Hellenic Diaspora* 27.1-2 (2001), 133-94.

van Steen, G., '"The World's a Circular Stage": Aeschylean Tragedy through the Eyes of Eva Palmer-Sikelianou', *International Journal of the Classical Tradition* 8.3 (2002), 375-93.

Vandvik, E., *The Prometheus of Hesiod and Aeschylus* (Oslo: Dybwad, 1943).

Vellacott, P. (tr.), *Aeschylus: Prometheus Bound and Other Plays* (Harmondsworth: Penguin, 1961).

Vlastos, G., 'On the Pre-History in Diodorus', *American Journal of Philology* 67.1 (1946), 51-9.

Vos, E., '*Prometheus* as Total Theatre: Production Notes', *Educational Theatre Journal* 22.1 (1970), 19-34.

Walton, J.M., *Found in Translation: Greek Drama in English* (Cambridge: Cambridge University Press, 2006).

Waterfield, R. (tr.), *The First Philosophers: The Presocratics and Sophists* (Oxford: Oxford University Press, 2000).

Weiss, P., *Die Verfolgung und Ermordung Jean Paul Marats dargestellt durch die Schauspielgruppe des Hospizes zu Charenton unter Anleitung des Herrn de Sade* (Frankfurt am Main: Suhrkamp Verlag, 1964).

Weiss, P., *The Persecution and Assassination of Marat as Performed by the Inmates of the Asylum of Charenton under the Direction of the Marquis of Sade* (London: Calder & Boyars, 1970), English version by Geoffrey Skelton; verse adaptation by Adrian Mitchell.

West, M.L. (ed.), *Hesiod. Theogony* (Oxford: Clarendon Press, 1966).

West, M.L. (ed.), *Hesiod. Works and Days* (Oxford: Clarendon Press, 1978).

West, M.L., 'The Prometheus Trilogy', *Journal of Hellenic Studies* 99 (1979), 130-48.

West, M.L. (ed.), *Aeschyli tragoediae, cum incerti poetae Prometheo* (Stuttgart: Teubner, 1990).

West, M.L., *Studies in Aeschylus* (Stuttgart: Teubner, 1990).

West, M.L. (ed.), *Iambi et elegi graeci ante Alexandrum cantati* (Oxford: Clarendon Press, 1989-92).

West, M.L. (tr.), *Hesiod: Theogony and Works and Days* (Oxford: Oxford University Press, 1998).

West, S.R., 'Herodotus' Portrait of Hecataeus', *Journal of Hellenic Studies* 111 (1991), 144-60.

Westphal, R., *Prolegomena zu Aeschylus Tragödien* (Leipzig: Teubner, 1869).

Whale, J., *Frankenstein* (Universal Pictures, 1931).

White, S., 'Io's World: Intimations of Theodicy in *Prometheus Bound*', *Journal of Hellenic Studies* 121 (2001), 107-40.

Wiles, D., *Greek Theatre Performance: An Introduction* (Cambridge: Cambridge University Press, 2000).

Winkler, J.J. and Zeitlin, F.I. (eds), *Nothing to do with Dionysos?* (Princeton: Princeton University Press, 1990).

Winnington-Ingram, R.P., 'The Danaid Trilogy of Aeschylus', *Journal of Hellenic Studies* 81 (1961), 141-52, a revised version printed in *Studies in Aeschylus*, 55-72.

Winnington-Ingram, R.P., *Studies in Aeschylus* (Cambridge: Cambridge University Press, 1983).

Woodson, T., 'Ahab's Greatness: Prometheus as Narcissus', *English Literary History* 33.3 (1966), 351-69.

Woot, P. de, *Should Prometheus be Bound? Corporate Global Responsibility* (Basingstoke: Palgrave Macmillan, 2009).

Wycherley, R.E., *The Stones of Athens* (Princeton: Princeton University Press, 1978).

Zeitlin, F.I., 'The Dynamics of Misogyny: Myth and Mythmaking in the *Oresteia*', *Arethusa* 11.1/2 (1978), 149-84.

Zuntz, G., 'Aeschyli Prometheus', *Harvard Studies in Classical Philology* 95 (1993), 107-11.

Chronology

Athenian arkhon years begin in early summer and are written, e.g., 459/8. As the dramatic festivals were held in late winter or early spring, plays took place in the second part of the year (so the *Oresteia* of 459/8 took place in spring 458, in our terms). Dates less than 1000 are all BCE (BC), those above 1000 are all CE (AD).

c. **525 BCE**: Aeschylus born.

514: Harmodios and Aristogeiton assassinate Hipparkhos, son of Peisistratos and brother of Hippias, tyrant of Athens.

510: End of the tyranny of the Peisistratids.

508/7: Reforms of Kleisthenes: beginning of Athenian democracy.

501/0: Institution of the board of generals (*stratêgoi*)

500/499: Aeschylus' first production.

499-4: Ionian Revolt.

490: Battle of Marathon.

488/7: First known use of ostracism.

481-79: Persian invasion: battles of Thermopylai, Artemision and Salamis (480), Plataia and Mykale (479).

478/7: Delian League formed.

473/2: Aeschylus' *Persians*.

469 (?): Battle of Eurymedon.

469/8: Sophokles wins first prize at his first performance.

468/7: Aeschylus' *Seven Against Thebes* (Oedipus trilogy).

465-3: Revolt of Thasos.

464/3 (?): Aeschylus' *Suppliant Women* (Danaid trilogy).

463 or 462: Kimon prosecuted (unsuccessfully). Kimon takes Athenian troops to Sparta.

462/1: Reforms of Ephialtes. Kimon returns and is ostracised. Alliance with Sparta broken. Athens allies with Argos and Thessaly.

460-59: 'First Peloponnesian War' begins. Battle of Halieis. Athens allies with Megara.

459/8: Aeschylus' *Oresteia*.

458/7: Areopagus opened to zeugites.

Chronology

457 (?): Battle of Tanagra. Battle of Oinophyta. Capture of Aigina.
458/7 or c. 455: Failure of the Egyptian expedition.
456/5: Aeschylus dies in Sicily.
454: Transfer of the treasury of the Delian League to Athens.
451/0: Perikles' citizenship law.
450: Death of Kimon on campaign in Cyprus.
447: Battle of Koroneia.
446: Revolt of Boiotia, Euboia and Megara. Thirty Year's Peace.
443: Foundation of Thourioi (Thurii).
c. 442: Sophokles' *Antigone*.
440-39: Samian Revolt
432/1: Outbreak of Peloponnesian War. Euripides' *Medea*.
431/0: Prosecution of Perikles; break in his continuous generalship.
430/29: Kratinos' *Wealth Gods*.
426/5: Aristophanes' *Akharnians*.
425/4: Aristophanes' *Knights*.
415: Launch of Sicilian expedition
415/4: Aristophanes' *Birds*.
413: Failure of Sicilian expedition
411: Oligarchic coup in Athens.
410: Restoration of democracy
406/5: Aristophanes' *Frogs*
404/3: Athens defeated in Peloponnesian War. Imposition of oligarchic regime.
403/2: Restoration of democracy.
338: Battle of Khaironeia; Macedonian supremacy.
323: Death of Alexander.
322: End of the radical Athenian democracy.
c. 300: Foundation of the Library at Alexandria.
1518 CE: First printed edition of Aeschylus.
1642-53: English Civil War (or English Revolution).
1649: Execution of Charles I.
  Establishment of the Commonwealth.
  Milton publishes *Eikonoklastes*.
1653: Oliver Cromwell becomes Lord Protector.
1658: Death of Oliver Cromwell.
1660: Restoration of monarchy.
1663: Stanley's edition of Aeschylus.
1664: *Paradise Lost* published.
1671: *Samson Agonistes* and *Paradise Regained* published.
1674: Second edition of *Paradise Lost* published.
1754: First printed Italian translations of Aeschylus.
1770: First printed French translation of Aeschylus.
1773: Goethe starts a play, *Prometheus*.
  First printed English translation of *Prometheus Bound*.

Chronology

1774: Goethe writes *Prometheus*.
1777: First full translation of Aeschylus in English.
1785: Unauthorised publication of Goethe's *Prometheus*.
1789: Goethe publishes *Prometheus*.
    French Revolution.
1815: Battle of Waterloo.
1816: Summer party at Villa Diodati. Mary Shelley conceives
    Frankenstein. Byron writes *Prometheus*.
1818: First edition of *Frankenstein*.
1819: Schubert sets Goethe's *Prometheus*.
1820: Percy Shelley publishes *Prometheus Unbound*.
1831: Third edition of *Frankenstein*.
1832: Great Reform Act.
1833: First version of *Prometheus Bound* by Elizabeth Barrett
    Browning.
1850: Second version of *Prometheus Bound* by Elizabeth Barrett
    Browning.
1899: André Gide, *Prométhée mal enchaîné*.
1917: Russian Revolution.
1927: Delphi Festival: Eva Palmer's *Prometheus Bound*.
1939-45: Second World War.
1945-9: Greek Civil War.
1967-74: Regime of the Colonels.
1968: Carl Orff's *Prometheus Bound*.
1981: Luigi Nono's *Prometeo: tragedia dell'ascolto*.
1997: Election of Labour government in the UK, led by Tony Blair.
1998: Tony Harrison, *Prometheus*.

Index

Index

Index

19734638R00101

Printed in Poland
by Amazon Fulfillment
Poland Sp. z o.o., Wrocław